Whe

THE PAST

Is Always

PRESENT

ROUTLEDGE PSYCHOSOCIAL STRESS SERIES
Charles R. Figley, Ph.D., Series Editor

When

THE PAST

Is Always

PRESENT

Emotional Traumatization, Causes, and Cures

RONALD A. RUDEN

Routledge
Taylor & Francis Group
New York   London

This book is part of the Psychosocial Stress Series, edited by Charles R. Figley.

Routledge
Taylor & Francis Group
711 Third Avenue,
New York, NY 10017

Routledge
Taylor & Francis Group
27 Church Road, Hove,
East Sussex BN3 2FA, UK

First issued in paperback 2014

Routledge is an imprint of the Taylor and Francis Group, an informa business

ISBN 978-0-415-87564-6 (hbk)
ISBN 978-1-138-87261-5 (pbk)

Library of Congress Cataloging-in-Publication Data

Ruden, Ronald A.
  When the past is always present : emotional traumatization, causes, and cures / Ronald A. Ruden. -- 1st ed.
    p. cm. -- (Psychosocial stress series)
    Includes bibliographical references and index.
    ISBN 978-0-415-87564-6 (hardcover : alk. paper)
    1. Psychic trauma. I. Title.

BF175.5.P75R83 2010
616.85'21--dc22   2010007844

Visit the Taylor & Francis Web site at
http://www.taylorandfrancis.com

and the Routledge Web site at
http://www.routledgementalhealth.com

For my wife and daughter,
Jax and Jamie, whose love is
the foundation of my life.

Contents

Series Editor's Foreword

For more than 40 years, starting with *Stress Disorders Among Vietnam Veterans* (1978), the Routledge (originally Brunner/Mazel) Psychosocial Stress Series has published important breakthroughs in the study and treatment of the traumatized.

The book *When the Past Is Always Present: Emotional Traumatization, Causes, and Cures* by Ronald Ruden, MD, PhD, an internist and clinical research scientist in New York City, is a welcomed and appropriate addition to the series. Ruden's work was familiar to me because of his theoretical treatises published in *Traumatology* between 2005 and 2009. Each were widely read and considered by the editorial board and ad hoc reviewer specialists to be significant contributions to an emerging field in the treatment of traumatization.

For the series, I suggested that Dr. Ruden formulate a book for the busy professional, so that practitioners would be able to pick up the book and quickly get the feel for what he had to say, and then be able use the therapeutic procedures he describes to help their clients. The publisher and I agree that Dr. Ruden has succeeded in this task.

Some who read this book will be incredulous, as were most of the reviewers for *Traumatology*, in the beginning. Eventually, the journal reviewers and those who reviewed the proposal for the book and this final version grasped the importance of this new paradigm and began to appreciate the positive implications of this orientation.

Dr. Ruden presents a neurobiological theory for the effectiveness of a type of exposure therapy that involves emotionally reexperiencing a trauma coupled with sensory stimulation. This theory synthesizes evolutionary biology with current neuroscience research and provides an explanation for the mysterious success of some odd and still controversial alternative therapies. Importantly, he offers suggestions for recognizing symptoms that could arise from a traumatization, and concludes that once recognized, a therapist should actively seek their traumatic origin so the event can be recalled and treated. Dr. Ruden then takes his findings one step further and suggests a new biologically consonant therapy he calls havening. This curious word, derived from the word *haven*, means to put into a safe place. Dr. Ruden and others believe that the ability to find a haven, while experiencing an intense emotional event, is at the core for both preventing and de-encoding a traumatic memory.

How is this accomplished? Why should this work? This book introduces the concept of psychosensory therapy, the use of sensory input to alter an emotionally traumatized brain. Before operationally defining traumatization, Dr. Ruden describes the conditions necessary and sufficient for a traumatic encoding moment. The consequences of this encoding are then illuminated. Dr. Ruden outlines in a general fashion the biology for curing a traumatization. He then specifically illustrates how applying havening fools the brain into believing a haven has been found, leading to a cure of the direct consequences of traumatization. For Dr. Ruden, a cure means that stimuli that had previously released stress chemicals and caused the reexperiencing of some or all of the encoded traumatic event are no longer able to do so. He does this without drugs or talk therapy.

The Psychosocial Stress Series, the oldest of its kind in the area of traumatic and systemic stress, welcomes this book with enthusiasm. While not the final word, it offers a different approach that will ultimately allow us to make traumatic memories a thing of the past.

Charles Figley, PhD
Series Editor
New Orleans, Louisiana

Foreword

A single concept is destined to dominate the field of psychotherapy for the rest of this century. That concept—emerging from profound breakthroughs in our understanding of the biological foundations of human emotion, thought, and motivation—is neuroplasticity. The brain is continually changing, learning, and evolving, and it is capable of changing itself in ways that could not even be imagined a few decades ago. As summarized by Columbia University neurologist Norman Doidge, MD: "The discovery that the human brain can change its own structure and function with thought and experience, turning on its own genes to change its circuitry, reorganize itself and change its operation, is the most important alteration in our understanding of the brain in four hundred years."

Freud's "talking cure" utilized insight and the uncovering of unconscious motivations, all within the container of the therapeutic relationship, with its transferences and countertransferences waiting to be analyzed. Sometimes this led to profound changes in behavior and life satisfaction. More often it just led to greater insight into the roots of one's misery. A hundred years later, we are able to identify many of the neurological shifts that are required to overcome depression, phobias, generalized anxiety disorders, obsessive-compulsive behavior, posttraumatic stress disorder (PTSD), and a host of other psychiatric maladies. Being able to facilitate desirable changes in the brain's chemistry trumps insight, willpower, and therapeutic rapport.

So the race is on. What therapies are able to most effectively, efficiently, and noninvasively shift the neurological underpinnings of problems people cannot overcome through willpower alone? Among the most promising of these new clinical modalities are descendents of Roger Callahan's Thought Field Therapy (TFT). By simply tapping on acupuncture points on the skin of traumatized patients while they were bringing to mind a distressful memory or trigger, something amazing seemed to occur. The memory or emotional trigger lost its ability to activate the fight-or-flight response that keeps people trapped in traumatic stress disorders. While initial case reports were met with tremendous skepticism, recent controlled trials support the early claims. Forty-seven of 50 Rwandan orphans who scored within the PTSD range 12 years after their parents were slaughtered in the genocide of 1994 were no longer above the PTSD cutoff after a single session of TFT according to caregiver ratings. Nor were they plagued by unrelenting nightmares, flashbacks, concentration difficulties, aggression, withdrawal, bed-wetting, or other symptoms of posttraumatic distress. Their improvements held on one-year follow-up. Abused male adolescents showed comparable improvement after a single session of tapping on acupuncture points, with 100% of the treatment group starting in the PTSD range and dropping below it after one treatment session. A wait-list comparison group showed no changes. Other studies are reporting similar findings.

How is this possible? That question has been engaging the fertile mind of the author of this book for the past half-dozen years. Dr. Ruden, a physician with a PhD in organic chemistry, worked early in his career with Nobel laureate E. J. Corey at Harvard, pioneering computer models of chemical synthesis. Now after three decades of practicing internal medicine and having established himself, with his book *The Craving Brain*, as one of the leading authorities on how advances in the neurosciences can bolster the treatment of disorders such as addictions and obesity, Dr. Ruden's career has taken an unconventional turn.

I met Dr. Ruden when he was newly into the approach discussed in this book. He confided to me that although he had established a substantial reputation for treating addictions rapidly and effectively, this new approach was producing stronger outcomes than anything else at his disposal. And it was deceptively simple to apply.

How can tapping on the body help people overcome long-standing, severe psychiatric disorders? The explanations that were being posed reached back thousands of years to acupuncture theory or postulated "thought fields" that cannot be detected or measured. Extraordinary results were being produced with no coherent scientific explanation. Dr. Ruden was deeply puzzled. This book is the fruit grown from that puzzlement.

With *When the Past Is Always Present: Emotional Traumatization, Causes, and Cures,* Dr. Ruden has done no less than to redraw the Eastern healing maps—written in the elusive ink of energy fields, energy centers, and energy pathways—with the neurologist's precise concepts and language for understanding therapeutic change. This monumental accomplishment will stand as the pioneering reference on the relevant neurochemical mechanisms as we move into a future where the techniques presented here become mainstays of psycho-therapy and healing. The first eight chapters provide a laudable first formulation of the neurological foundations of trauma-based disor-ders, their cure, and how the methods featured bring about that cure with unprecedented effectiveness.

The ways to apply these methods, the best protocols, and the nec-essary ingredients are all areas of controversy. The original approach used specific acupuncture points. It stimulated them by tapping them in a given order. Now more than two dozen discrete variations have been developed, each with its own proponents, literature, and train-ing programs. Many still use acupuncture points, although not nec-essarily those originally prescribed, nor are they tapped in the order that was originally suggested. In fact, some no longer use tapping, or acupuncture points for that matter. Some focus on other energy systems familiar to Eastern healing and spiritual traditions, such as the chakras or the aura. Some believe that almost any innocuous sen-sory stimulation, combined with the mental activation of a problem or a goal, can lead to desirable neurological change. Dr. Ruden enters his preferred approach, called havening, into the ring with this book. It is built upon his experimentation with numerous formulations in treating literally thousands of patients. Perhaps the most interesting thing about these approaches, however, is not whether or not havening is better than the others, but that they all seem to obtain similarly strong results. One day research studies will have distinguished the most important elements in the almost unbelievable effectiveness of these methods, but this book already provides strong and illuminating hypotheses for how they impact the brain.

David Feinstein, PhD
Ashland, Oregon

Preface

To permanently eliminate chronic physical and emotional pain without drugs or surgery, literally in minutes, where all else has failed, should be considered under the heading of "miraculous." At the core of these miracles, I believe, is the ability to erase the emotional response to a traumatic event. Is this really possible? Until recently, traumatization encoded enduring memories, emotions, and sensations in our mind and body that produced lifelong distress. Because of the way a traumatization is embedded, we are often at a loss to understand why our thoughts, feelings and even our physical bodies behave the way they do. The lack of awareness as to the origin of these problems is of enormous import as it prevents individuals and healthcare providers from considering that the symptoms and behaviors are of traumatic origin. This leads to unnecessary suffering as traditional therapeutic interventions almost always fail.

Herein we describe a therapy that cures suffering arising from trauma. It is rapid and has no side effects. It can be self-applied. Like the ancient shaman[1] and the modern faith healer,[2] it uses touch and other sensory input as one of its primary therapeutic tools. While Western medicine views these somatic therapies with skepticism, I know that it works.

This therapy arose from research seeking to uncover the neurobiology of tapping, a therapeutic approach first described by Dr. Roger Callahan[3] and further developed by Gary Craig.[4] Tapping, literally tapping, on acupuncture points after recalling an emotional event produced remarkable relief for both psychological and physical problems. Uncovering the neuroscience behind tapping has led to a therapy called **havening**. *Havening*, the transitive verb of the word *haven*, means to put in a safe place. During havening, our responses to stimuli that remind us of the trauma are changed forever. In its most basic form, havening is a process that involves three phases. First is the generation of affect by cognitive retrieval of the event or one of its components. Second is a special form of touch, havening touch, comforting and soothing, applied after retrieval of the memory. Havening touch is intermixed with other forms of touch, such as tapping. Third, accompanying the havening touch, the individual follows a set of instructions designed to distract. Each phase plays a role in extinguishing the consequences of traumatization and freeing us from the chains of remembrance. The moment this is accomplished, one is havened.

This book describes the process and conditions necessary to encode an event as a traumatic memory. Understanding this allows us to more readily diagnose certain symptoms as arising from a traumatic event. For example, one should consider that a painful condition is the result of a traumatization if there is no evidence for a recent injury, if the pain is nonanatomical in distribution, and if the response to traditional therapy is poor. Certain psychological conditions, such as phobias, panic disorder, and of course, posttraumatic stress disorder, alert us to the probability of a traumatic origin. A history of an unresolved, highly emotional event makes the diagnosis of a trauma-related disorder more likely. Seeking the earliest recollection of symptoms and even earlier events that may have set the stage for the traumatization is necessary. This requires thoughtful and recursive questioning.

To Western eyes, havening therapy might appear bizarre, but to watch pain instantly disappear, psychological problems resolve, and disturbing memories fade into the irretrievable past is nothing short of astonishing. While some forms of this therapy have been around for over two decades, many mental health professionals remain skeptical, given that it involves no medication, talking, or prolonged exposure to the original traumatizing event. It is certainly at odds with currently accepted biological principles of healing. It is hoped that putting this therapy within a neurobiological framework will open the way for acceptance of these new methods of healing.

Notes and References

1. The term *shaman* is believed to have originated among the Siberian Tungus (Evenks) over 30,000 years ago. The literal translation of shaman is "he (or she) who knows."
2. Randi, J. (1989). *The faith healers*. Amherst, NY: Prometheus Books.
3. Callahan, R. (1985). *The five-minute phobia cure*. Wilmington, DE: Enterprise. Retrieved from www.tftrx.com
4. Craig, G. *Emotional freedom techniques*. Retrieved from www.emofree.com

Acknowledgments

I am grateful to Dr. Paul McKenna, who six years ago asked whether I had heard of Dr. Callahan's approach for the treatment of psychological problems that involved tapping on various parts of the body and face. I hadn't. His direction led me to read several books on the method, and I later spoke with several practitioners, including Mary Sise, MSW, then president of the Association for Comprehensive Energy Psychology (ACEP), and Steven Reed, PhD, a psychotherapist from Texas. I was intrigued and curious to understand how this therapy worked.

During the course of my research I encountered Dr. Joaquin Andrade, an internist with training in traditional Chinese medicine from Uruguay, and one of the authors of a paper discussing the use of this therapy with 29,000 patients over 14 years. He, along with his colleagues Dr. Christine Sutherland and Dr. Martin Alberese, guided my early thinking about this therapy. I also had the good fortune to discuss this methodology and other ideas with Dr. David Feinstein, the other author of that paper.

I began exploring the research on conditioned fear and its extinction. Researchers such as Joseph LeDoux, James McGaugh, Denis Pare, Karem Nader, Michael Fanselow, Elizabeth Phelps and others provided useful neurobiological data. Later, as the de-traumatization hypothesis described here was being formulated, the clinical literature by Bessel A. van der Kolk, Mark E. Bouton, Onno van der Hart, Peter Levine, Robert Scaer, and others offered insights into the consequences of traumatic stress. I am particularly appreciative to Dr. Scaer for personally sharing his thoughts and work with me. The research carried out by these brilliant scientists is outlined in this book.

Through hours of patient contact, reading, and discussion with other individuals, I was able to formulate a potentially useful model on why tapping works. By far the most important was my brother, Dr. Steven Ruden. He, too, was amazed at what he was able to do and contributed much to my understanding. My colleagues Vera Mehta, PhD, Vera Vento, MSW, and Barbara Barnum, RN, PhD, also read many versions of this manuscript and were insightful and encouraging. These discussions led me to formulate a new approach, which I call havening.

Also of great importance was my spouse, Jacalyn Barnett, who as every author knows, had to deal with the obsessive determination needed to complete the task. I am beyond grateful to her for making our home a place where I could do this. Marcia Byalick superbly line edited the manuscript, making it more readable. Steve Lampasona (lampasona@earthlink.net) is the talented artist who provided many of the book's images and the cover. Clara Joinson, my editor while developing the manuscript that was presented to the publisher, was instrumental in helping me clarify my thinking. Anna Moore, my editor at Routledge, guided this project with a loving hand. She gave the manuscript to Dr. Mel Harper, a brilliant researcher whose investigations involve understanding how trauma is de-encoded within the brain. His review was illuminating, to say the least. He helped add precision and an additional view, that of electrical de-potentiation, making the work richer and clearer. Judith Simon, my senior editor at Taylor and Francis, displayed uncommon patience with the continued revisions of this book. Dr. Charles Figley, as editor-in-chief of the journal *Traumatology*, provided a forum for my early efforts and was invaluable in encouraging Routledge to publish the book.

Finally, I thank my patients, who generously provided feedback as to what worked and what didn't. Their trust allowed me to experiment and explore.

Author's Note

This book speculates about how and why emotionally reexperiencing a traumatic event coupled with the simple laying on of hands and other sensory input can cure trauma-based illness. The content is primarily for clinicians, but lay readers may also find it of interest. It is not an academic book in the traditional sense; rather, it is a primer that introduces a neurobiological theory on how trauma is encoded and gives practical advice on how to cure its consequences. While clinicians will be readily able to apply these methods, untrained individuals may also be able to self-administer these techniques for simple problems. For individuals suffering from complex trauma, it is best to work with a trained therapist.

Throughout this book is information that is somewhat technical in nature and highlighted in bold italics. Examples and illustrative stories within the body of the text are italicized. Bolded text indicates the introduction of a new term; these terms can be found in the glossary. In addition, bold text is used for emphasis.

This book uses references directly from the Internet because they are easily accessible by readers. One reference that has been useful in providing overviews of topics is Wikipedia, the free online encyclopedia. Appendix I provides notes and additional references for the interested reader.

A THIRD PILLAR

This chapter introduces a group of therapies that treats emotional and physical disorders encoded in the brain as a result of traumatization. We term this group the **psychosensory** therapies. This term ties together techniques that have long since been introduced by others. It is suggested here that the psychosensory therapies be included along with the psychotherapies and psychopharmacology as one of three pillars for the treatment of physical and emotional suffering. While language in the psychotherapies and drugs in psychopharmacology are the tools that are used to produce change for these two pillars, it is the **extrasensory response** to sensory input that effects change in psychosensory therapy. In the psychosensory therapy **havening**, touch produces the change. It is not just the simple act of touch and the brain's concomitant response that is therapeutic; it is the meaning the brain ascribes to the touch that appears to be critical.

Memories are the stuff we are made of. They consist of acquired knowledge, the forms, faces, and personalities of people we have met, things we have seen, and things we can do. There are memories that provide pleasure, and others that cause pain. We are traumatized when, reminded of a painful memory, we reexperience the original emotions and feelings.

Traumatization Appears to Produce Immutable Feelings, Thoughts, and Behaviors as if Written in Stone

You cannot find a safe place. Everywhere you go there is danger and distress. You wish for safety and seek it continually, but it never comes, for there is no rest without a haven. Anita, the granddaughter of a Holocaust survivor, won't leave home without a loaf of bread in her purse. Every night before going to sleep Sarah checks under her bed for snakes. Marty has suffered from a nonstop headache for two years. Rosa panics whenever she leaves her home. Josie worries about low-flying planes crashing into her apartment. John's left nostril has been congested for seven years. For these individuals, this is life following their traumatization. Strange behaviors, unremitting pain, extraordinary physical sensations, and irrational fears are the consequences of the pathological brain-mind-behavior-body connections caused by traumatization. These abnormal connections produce distress beyond words. What causes this to happen? How does it happen? Why doesn't it get better? While there are currently few answers, two facts are secure: Traumatization changes the individual, and the place where the change takes place is the brain.

Traumatization Always Involves Intense Emotions

We remember things because they are associated with strong feelings. There is no traumatization without them. Yet our entire life is filled with emotional events that aren't traumatizing. What is unique about a traumatizing event? Ultimately, traumatization is about being trapped in the uncompleted act of escape. Here, in this book, we will describe a method to help the traumatized escape from the inescapable and find a safe haven. It is here, in this safe place, that our response to the memory of the event is changed forever.

How does one gain entry into the brain systems encoding those memories that produce abnormal behavior, thoughts, emotions, and feelings so they might be altered? We offer the **psychosensory therapies** as another approach, a third pillar (along with the two current pillars, the psychotherapies and psychopharmacologies) if you will, to change our response to these memories. To understand why the psychosensory therapies deserve to be called a third pillar, a brief review of the two current therapies is necessary.

The First Pillar: The Psychotherapies

Lady Macbeth's physician failed. He could only watch as she sleepwalked, rubbing her hands, trying to remove the "damned spot" of the murdered king's blood. Aware this behavior was beyond his understanding, he was nonetheless prescient when he commented, "Infected minds to their deaf pillows will discharge their secrets."[1] The physician who spoke Shakespeare's words was referring to what happens during sleep. Three hundred years later Freud[2] listened to those secrets in the imaginary world of sleep, in stories we call dreams. Dreams, Freud declared, were the "royal road to the unconscious" that led to where the infection lay buried. By bringing these memories to conscious awareness and analyzing them, the unconscious would yield its secrets, thus uncovering both their origin and an approach to treating the problem. This could be accomplished, according to Freud, by talking with a trained professional who helped decipher the metaphorical clues in dreams. His ideas are described in his 1899 book *The Interpretation of Dreams*. Other early researchers, including Jung[3] and Janet,[4] also dug into the dreams arising during sleep to find the moment of traumatic encoding.

Over the last century, various methods for talking to patients as a way of treating problems became grouped into an approach called the **psychotherapies**. By using language, as in conversation, it was hoped the response patterns to memories could be altered. The pillar of psychotherapy attempts to deal with distressing emotions arising from life experiences.[5] In general, most practitioners use the problem-cure model. The goal is to help the individual understand the origin of his or her feelings and reframe them so that they are no longer distressful. Psychotherapy uses only spoken conversation and occurs within a structured context. I do not know any talk therapy that encourages the therapist to touch the patient. In fact, it is generally forbidden—the cordial shaking of hands being the only exception. Research reveals that the quality of the relationship between the therapist and the client has a greater influence on client outcomes than the specific type of therapy used by the therapist. Below are listed several systems of psychotherapy.

Cognitive behavioral
Person centered
Psychodynamic
Psychoanalytic
Rational/emotive
Systemic (including family therapy)

The Second Pillar: The Psychopharmacologies

Decades later, armed with research showing that thought, mood, and behavior were a function of the amount and types of chemicals in the brain, physicians attempted to heal the mind by altering the brain's chemistry. It was found that different substances (drugs) entering our bodies, by either ingestion or injection, could correct an imbalance of these chemicals. By doing so, symptoms arising from these abnormal levels could be ameliorated. These drugs, instead of reframing the underlying problem, restored normal levels of the chemicals needed for information processing, which in turn changed how we felt. For most symptoms, if the underlying issues are not resolved, the beneficial effect of the drug lasts only as long as the substance remains in the brain.

Psychopharmacology[6] is the study and use of chemicals to change mood, sensation, thinking, and behavior. The brain is a complex chemical soup. Dozens of substances are found to influence information processing and perception. The consequences of chemical imbalances include most of the disorders we consider psychological in nature, such as anxiety, depression, paranoia, and bipolar disorder. Thus, we have antianxiety drugs, antidepressant drugs, drugs that help us focus better, drugs that inhibit compulsive behavior, drugs that stop hallucinations, drugs that help us sleep, and drugs that help keep us awake. There are no drugs proven to cure a traumatization.

In psychopharmacology, the therapeutic relationship between the drug prescriber and the drug taker is of little consequence. The patient relates the effect of the drug, and the therapist adjusts the medications accordingly. This approach does not deal with the causes of the problem; rather, it relies on a diagnosis based on the manifestations in thought, behavior, and mood, which in turn, we have learned, reflect levels of the neurochemicals. This then leads to the choice of drugs. Below are listed some psychopharmacological drug classes.

Antidepressants
Antianxiety
Anticompulsive

Antihallucinatory
Mood stabilizers
Pain relievers

Given the complexity of the brain, it is indeed remarkable that medications can truly be of help.

The Third Pillar: The Psychosensory Therapies

This book proposes a third pillar. This pillar comprises those therapies that use various forms of sensory input to alter brain function. We call this third pillar the **psychosensory therapies**, a body-mind approach. We argue that the psychosensory therapies, by using sensory input to restore dysfunctional systems to healthier function, represent a third pillar for the treatment of psychologically based problems, as they produce change by a **different mechanism** than the two previous pillars. Since sensory input has no inherent psychological component, we seek to explore those **extrasensory responses** to sensory input that allow for healing. We define an extrasensory response as one that arises, unbidden from sensory input.

It is not surprising that sensory input can alter the brain. For example, we can experience joy when listening to music, craving when passing a bar, or comfort when being massaged. In fact, we experience extrasensory responses all day long. Whether smelling the chicken soup wafting out from a restaurant, stroking a pet, or enjoying a beautiful sunset, our senses evoke responses beyond those of simple sensory input. We take for granted all that happens to us during our hectic daily routine, and many of us miss the opportunity to use what we touch, see, hear, taste, and smell to make us happier and calmer, literally not stopping for that moment to "smell the roses." While the mechanisms by which sensory input produces these extrasensory responses are not well understood, it must somehow involve the "meaning," learned or innate, of the input to the organism.

Some psychosensory therapies produce a permanent change, while others require long-term maintenance therapy. A partial list of the psychosensory therapies is given below, and a fuller, but brief, discussion can be found in Chapter 9.

Group 1
    Havening
    Emotional Freedom Techniques (EFT)
    Callahan Techniques–Thought Field Therapy (CT-TFT)
    Eye movement desensitization and reprocessing (EMDR)

Group 2
    Yoga
    Acupuncture
    Biofeedback/neurofeedback
    Exercise and related activities
    Music
    Light
    Aromatherapy
    Massage
    Reiki
    Rolfing

Psychosensory therapies can be grouped into two major divisions, one in which the mind is activated by the memory of the event or a component of the event just prior to sensory input, and one in which the mind is at rest prior to sensory input. The first group is mind activated and addresses life-specific events and places them in a category called exposure therapies. The second group acts more generally to downregulate stress and its impact on information processing.

The specific event therapies are very similar in that they require a component of the event to be brought to conscious awareness. This book explores havening. A brief discussion of EFT, CT-TFT, and EMDR is given later; however, it is likely that similar mechanisms are at work for these four therapies.

Can we use the **extrasensory responses** of sensory input to alleviate suffering arising from a deeply rooted sorrow? To change our subconscious? It is our goal to begin to answer these questions. We will show that psychosensory therapies, including havening, have in fact a solid neurobiological basis. By the end of this book, I hope to have proven that the use of sensory input to treat trauma-based disorders is indeed a third pillar and worthy of study.

We begin by exploring the question: What it is about emotions that is necessary for traumatization, and further, why do we have emotions and what are they good for?

References

1. Shakespeare, W. (1603). *Macbeth* (Act V, Scene 1).
2. Freud, S. (1899). *The interpretation of dreams*. Vienna, Austria: Franz Deuticke.
3. Jung, C. (1947). *On the nature of the psyche. Collected works* (Vol. 8). London, UK: Routledge and Kegan Paul.
4. Janet, P. (1925). *Psychological healing: A historical and clinical study* (2 vols., E. Paul & C. Paul, Trans.). London, UK: George Allen & Unwin.
5. Wikipedia. *Psychotherapy*. Retrieved December 12, 2008, from http://en.wikipedia.org/wiki/Psychotherapy
6. Wikipedia. *Psychopharmacology*. Retrieved December 12, 2008, from http://en.wikipedia.org/wiki/Psychopharmacology

2

THE ROLE EMOTIONS PLAY

What are emotions? Why are they important? What role do emotions play in memory? What role do they play in survival and traumatization?

Types of Emotions

Emotions are everything. They personalize our life. Without them our past fades into the realm of high school chemistry and college calculus. Since we have them, we must ask: What evolutionary advantage do they confer? What role do they play in improving our chances of survival? And finally, what is their role in traumatization?

Ortony, Norman, and Revelle[1] propose that emotions are generated on three levels: reactive, routine, and reflective. The most primitive are **reactive**; hardwired and innate. These emotions are **fear** and **defensive rage**, and they are produced in response to a perceived threat. From birth, for human and other mammals, fear can be generated by the appropriate stimulus, and the response is stereotypical. Later in life, rage appears. Fear and rage energize us to flee or fight. Both emotions activate the requisite physiology that ensures, to the best of our abilities, we survive to the next day.

We go in and out of **routine** emotions such as happiness, sadness, surprise, and anger daily. They nourish our lives, lasting for a while, then fading, only to give rise to other emotions. Psychologists who study these emotions have estimated that humans experience about 30 or more different emotional states every day. Sometimes we can experience many emotions is a short period of time.

It was a most extraordinary day. The spaceship Challenger had on board a teacher, an ordinary teacher who was going to explore space with the astronauts. Schools set up TVs in auditoriums; friends and family of Christa McAuliffe were being photographed live at Cape Kennedy. The liftoff went

9

smoothly and fingers shook with excitement, pointing at the rising space-
ship. This lasted 73 seconds, until inexplicably there was an explosion. What
happened? Hands came down and eyes just stared. It was quiet. Confusion
was followed by bewilderment, uncertainty, anxiety, emotions cascading,
one after another. Then, they just stood there, not knowing.

Some Daily Routine Emotions

Adoring	Agitated	Agreeable	Confused	Cool	Happy	
Sweet	Sunny	Paralyzed	Tender	Shy	Puzzled	
Annoyed	Eager	Inspired	Brave	Selfish	Worried	Calm

Finally, there are emotions that are **reflective** in nature. They
require conscious thought and include anger, guilt, shame, hatred,
grief, jealousy, love, revenge, and others. They, like reactive emotions,
have the potential to be traumatically encoded and thus sustained over
time. These divisions are clearly not absolute since overlap occurs.

These three types of emotional states—reactive, routine, and reflective—arise from different parts of the brain. Reactive, the most survival-
based emotion, originates in the **limbic system** (see page 23), the part of
the brain we share with all mammals. The routine emotions originating
in the sensory parts of the brain do not require thought; they just occur
as a matter of course. The reflective emotions involve the most advanced
part of our brains, the **prefrontal lobe**. It is here that evaluation takes
place. While these emotions are considered by some scientists to be
uniquely human, animals can exhibit behavior that suggests they, too,
experience grief, jealousy, and other reflective emotions.

Emotions Are Stressors

All events that generate emotions act as stressors; that is, they change
the levels of specific chemicals in our brain. Even though we are speaking primarily of negative emotions, it is important to remember that
positive emotions act as stressors as well. As most emotions are fleeting, they do not affect us over the long term. However, when an event
is encoded as a traumatization, it has the potential to last a lifetime.
Since all traumatizations involve distressful emotions, and a traumatically encoded emotion does not diminish over time, a traumatized

event produces chronic inescapable stress, a permanent imbalance. The inability of the brain to restore normal balance sets the stage for further traumatization and generates symptoms that are maladaptive. We use the word *traumatized* to denote an event or feeling that has been pathologically and permanently encoded. A traumatized event, as we shall see, produces unique changes in the brain and leads to what clinicians and scientists call a traumatic memory.

Reactive and reflective emotions generally do not feel good, and we want to avoid them, if possible. They are part of what is called the aversive survival system. This system activates fear and rage during threatening events where outrunning or outfighting a predator is required. Fear is also activated to prevent us from doing something that might produce guilt, shame, rage and other distressing emotions. This helps keep our society intact.

In addition to situational events, another survival system takes care of our recurring daily appetitive needs, driving us to seek food, water, and sex. This system motivates by producing feelings of hunger, thirst, and sexual desire that act as stressors. The longer the need is unmet, the greater the stress; the greater the stress, the greater the motivation. These drives make up the appetitive survival system. These two systems are interconnected and have similar goals. They both increase our chances for survival. It is not surprising that in disorders involving abnormal appetitive drives such as addiction or compulsive eating, a traumatized or inherently abnormal reactive or reflective emotion, acting as a stressor, is often found at its core.

The Relationship Between the Aversive and Appetitive Survival Systems

For the mammalian class, there are two major systems driving survival. One is the positively valenced appetitive system, which includes internal homeostatic *processes that make us seek food, water, sex, and attachment. These systems drive behavior by producing pain and longing and manifest as hunger, thirst, sexual desire, and loneliness. Pain reduction, achieved by accomplishing a learned task (e.g., getting food and eating it), is often pleasurable, and the pain-pleasure cycle never ceases. In the normal cycle you get hungry, you seek food, you eat food, you get full and you get hungry again sometime in the future. After eating, you are in a refractory period, no longer motivated by the sight or thought of food as the pain of hunger is removed. This makes sense, as you would have no time left to do other things if you were always driven to eat.*

The second major system is the negatively valenced aversive system. This is designed to help us avoid danger, and if unable to do so, then try to find a way to escape. It increases our ability to store and retrieve memories of threatening events so that we are alerted to similar circumstances. Once activated, it manifests with the experiences of vigilance, fear, panic, rage, and in some cases, flaccidity or passing out. Both the appetitive and aversive systems use distressful feelings, such as hunger or fear, respectively, to motivate behavior.

The word emotion is derived from the Latin emovere, meaning "to move out," suggesting action; early uses of the term referred to a moving, stirring, or physical agitation. Emotions are the primary motivational systems for both sets of drives, as Tompkins[2] observes: "Without its amplification, nothing matters, and with its amplification, anything can matter. It combines urgency and generality. It lends power to memory, to perception, to thought and to action." If the relief of a sensation, such as fear or hunger is not accomplished, the organism enters a period of chronic stress.

Incredibly complex networks that monitor internal and external stimuli modulate these two survival systems. The two areas of the brain that drive these survival behaviors are the **nucleus accumbens**[3] *for appetitive drives and the* **amygdala**[4] *for aversive emotions. These systems are interconnected and are modulated by the evaluative portion of our brain, the prefrontal cortex.[5]*

There is sense to how these systems set up and shut down in the nontraumatized person. When engaged, both systems increase salience and vigilance; that is, they increase the importance and urgency of the object to the individual seeking it, and thereby make clues to its whereabouts stand out. Odor arising from food or a predator, perception of movement and sound are such sensory inputs requiring increased salience for survival. **Dopamine** *and* **norepinephrine,** *primitive neurochemicals, enhance our observations and make stimuli more noticeable.[6] When hungry we want to be able to smell food or follow a trail that leads to nourishment. When anxiety is cued, we want to focus on the presence* *of a potential predator. Dopamine and norepinephrine both arouse and motivate us to action for both systems, they also enhance learning.*

When we do not need to seek food or worry about predators, serotonin is released. Elevated levels cause us to feel safe and sated. Salience and vigilance are quieted. Nature is very economical in its mechanisms and methods.

Emotional Awareness

On occasion, we experience fear for reasons that are not brought to conscious awareness. The emotion of fear can be produced by subconscious stimuli, a sense that something is not right. We feel uneasy, yet we can't put our finger on it.[7] It makes us pay more attention to our surroundings and try to determine what is making us anxious. The absence of fear allows for socialization, creative thought, sexual pursuits, and other pleasurable activities, such as eating and sleeping.

Emotions Are Motivating and Aid With Decisions

Motivation is another use for emotions. What one does for love is an example. This motivation can produce great art or horrible crimes. Decision making is modulated by emotions. It can be self-evident or it can be subtle when we make a decision based on feeling. Emotions alert us when a personal decision just doesn't feel right. Not only do emotions alert us to wrong decisions, but they help in diminishing the choices we present to our conscious awareness. This subconscious pruning of options must be present so we can negotiate our complex culture without weighing in on each and every option. It is amazing that Spock, the Vulcan chief science officer of *Star Trek* fame, never used emotions to calculate the best course of action. Captain James T. Kirk knew what felt right and acted.

Emotions as Physical Forms of Communication

Emotions provide a survival value by being a form of communication. Darwin[8] noted that emotions are writ large on the body, producing involuntary posturing, a dog's wagging tail, hair standing on end, and in humans, facial expressions. It is by reading the outward signs of these inner feelings that we can respond appropriately. Facial expressions for reactive and routine emotions are easy to read and are universal. Our recognition of these expressions is hardwired, and interestingly, by observing them, they can produce in us similar feelings. This allows us to more rapidly learn their meaning. Researchers have recently described a special group of mirror neurons that appear to mediate this process (see Appendix A). Most of the time, seeing someone crying stirs emotions within us. Seeing someone joyous activates us as well. This emotional process aids us in learning how other people feel. We can sense when a person is lying to us. It is why we have a trial by a jury. Sometimes, however, facial expressions can be used to confuse us.

In addition, there is an interesting mind-body loop.[9] If we activate just the anatomy of an emotion, say, making a happy smile, it feeds back to the brain and makes us feel the emotional underpinnings. Not necessarily as strong, but definitely recognizable. As we shall see later on, fear and defensive rage are characterized by certain physiological postures. If we act out the opposite of the usual bodily response to an emotion, we are often able to control our emotion. A simple experiment is illustrative. Try to feel anger with a slack jaw and closed lips while breathing normally through your nose. It is quite difficult, and indeed for some, impossible. This observation, which has potential for anger management, will be discussed in more detail later.

Emotions Involved With Social Bonding

Emotions are also associated with social bonding. Maternal love and fealty, kinship, friendship, and the sharing of a common goal are all driven by emotions. Fealty, in particular the loyalty toward a superior or comrade, as in a fighting unit, is a powerful force. These emotions are the glue that binds strangers into an army, a community, a culture, or a nation. It produces attachment and helps protect all of us.

Emotions and Memory

Emotions facilitate the storage of memory, making it easier to retrieve.[10] It is as if emotions are a yellow highlighter for memory. If we experienced fear during a situation, it would be important to remember so that in the future we could avoid similar circumstances. Emotions not only facilitate memory storage and retrieval, but they also modulate the formation of associative bonds to event-related components.

In summary, emotions, the sum of feeling and physiology, have survival value. They increase our ability to store survival information, prepare us to ward off predators, allow for communication, motivate us, bind us together, and let us know if we are doing the right thing. The basic emotions are innate, not learned. They enable animals, including humans, to more effectively negotiate their environments, eat, drink, mate, make decisions, and defend themselves. The physical and feeling states of emotions result from electrochemical activity in the brain. It is this activity that affects the way we process our environment, how it is perceived, encoded, stored, and retrieved. Stimuli that produce emotions critical to survival also set the stage for traumatization. It should come as no surprise that those stimuli causing fear and defensive rage are of the greatest importance.

References

1. Ortony, A., Norman, D. A., & Revelle, W. (2005). Affect and proto-affect in effective functioning. In J.-M. Fellous & M. A. Arbib (Eds.), *Who needs emotions: The brain meets the robot.* (pp. 173–202). New York, NY: Oxford University Press.

2. Tompkins, S. S. (1982). Affect theory. In P. Eckman (Ed.), *Emotion in the human face* (p. 355). As quoted by Kelly, A. E., Neurochemical networks encoding emotion and motivation. In J.-M. Fellous & M. A. Arbib (Eds.), *Who needs emotion: The brain meets the robot* (p. 34). New York, NY: Oxford University Press.

3. Nicola, S. M., Yun, I. A., Wakabayashi, K. T., & Fields, H. L. (2004). Firing of nucleus accumbens neurons during the consummatory phase of a discriminative stimulus task depends on previous reward predictive cues. *J. Neurophysiol.* 91:1866–1882.
   Wikipedia. *Nucleus accumbens.* Retrieved January 7, 2009, from http://en.wikipedia.org/wiki/Nucleus_Accumbens

4. Hamann, S. B., Ely, T. D., Grafton, S. T., & Kilts, C. D. (1999). Amygdala activity related to enhanced memory for pleasant and aversive stimuli. *Nature Neurosci.* 2:289–293.
   Wikipedia. *Amygdala.* Retrieved January 30, 2010, from http://en.wikipedia.org/wiki/Amygdala

5. Wikipedia. *Prefrontal cortex.* Retrieved January 7, 2009, from http://en.wikipedia.org/wiki/Prefrontal_cortex

6. Fellous, J.-M., & Suri, R. E. (2002). The roles of dopamine. In M. A. Arbib (Ed.), *Handbook of brain theory and neural networks* (2nd ed.). Cambridge, MA: MIT Press.
Ventura, R., Morrone, C., & Puglisi-Allegra, S. (2007). Prefrontal/accumbal catecholamine system determines motivational salience attribution to both reward and aversion-related stimuli. *Proc. Natl. Acad. Sci.* 104:5181–5186.
7. DeBecker, G. (1997). *The gift of fear*. New York, NY: Little Brown & Company.
8. Darwin, C. (1898). *The expression of the emotions in man and animals*. New York, NY: Appleton and Company.
9. Wikipedia. Emotion. Retrieved May 3, 2010 from http://en.wikipedia.org/wiki/Emotion
10. Reisberg, D., & Hertel, P. (Eds.). (2004). *Memory and emotion*. New York, NY: Oxford University Press.

3

ANCIENT EMOTIONS AND SURVIVAL

Fear and rage are critical for survival because they activate our body and mind, preparing us to respond to a perceived threat. How are these emotions generated? The answer lies in an area of the brain called the amygdala.

Fear and Survival

Tot's hair bristled: It was standing straight up. He knew he had wandered away from his mother, but the strange sounds had intrigued him. Vigilance versus curiosity. But now there was a problem because he didn't like that familiar odor. He smelled hungry predators and he was their prey. They were hyena, a mean bunch and smart, too. He knew he was in trouble. Those ancient feelings of fear had arisen to warn him, to tell him to run, but now he could not. His legs were scared stiff and he was stuck. The hyenas encircled him. His muscles tensed and as he rose up on his hind legs, he let out the best roar a young pup could. But the hyenas kept closing in. There was no escape. Tot ran in circles. The alpha male hyena was coming in for the kill, saliva already dripping from his mouth. The hyena suddenly looked up and there was Tot's mother, the largest lion cat he had ever seen. His saliva dried up, and as she leapt to protect her son, he ran, as did the others of his pack. With a roar that shook the trees, Tot's mother cuddled her son and they returned to the pride.

We all have fear hardwired in us. The open plain feels unsafe alone. Entering a dark, tight cave dries the mouth. A dark, rumbling roar sets the head in that direction.

Fear is the most ancient of emotions. It can be generated without conscious awareness. It is what makes us jump when something

17

moves on the ground or rubs against the bottom of our leg. It makes us duck when we see something out of the corner of our eye, and it makes us run and hide, even if we are not yet aware of what the threat is. We jump, duck, run, or hide because sensory input has driven us straight into action. The patterns that motivate this response are older, much older than the human race. Much older than the thinking part of the brain. It is because of this response, however, that species have survived. Avoiding predation is something we witness, if we are aware, every day. For example, mosquitoes put their lives at stake to get blood; if they are to succeed, they must respond rapidly and correctly to avoid being squished.

Fear is personal. It makes you focus. No emotion supersedes it. It is conserved throughout all of evolution. Although we may not characterize a slug responding with avoidance to a hot flame as experiencing fear, it is the action of fear.

Fear has many moments. There is the moment of awareness. We experience a subtle, heightened sense of our surroundings, vigilance, telling us something is not right. We try to localize the fear-inducing stimulus, scanning the horizon for trouble, looking for unusual motion; scents or sounds of a potential predator become salient. If we sense something, we freeze, facing the direction of the stimulus. This freezing serves two purposes: to avoid motion so that the predator cannot see us and to allow us to focus. It is mildly activating. If we cannot discern a cause for concern, we return to what we were doing. Sometimes, however, we rationalize and shrug it off, and this can be to our peril.

At first one gazelle picked up his head from the grazing grass and scanned the horizon. What was that smell? The wind was gently flowing from the forest to the plain but nothing was moving save the grass. What was that smell? Another gazelle also picked up his head. Was it in response to the first, or was it something that he had detected? Now the focus was on the edge of the forest. Other gazelles also lifted their heads and scanned the area. Nothing? Nothing. They continued to feed and the vigilance dissipated.

Then there is the fear in the moment of danger, such as being chased by a predator. We are in full flight mode. This signal is sent from body to mind and mind to body. Our muscles become stronger, our heart beats harder and faster, our pupils dilate to see better—a struggle for survival is about to begin. We think about escape. Where can one hide? In a moment of perceived danger, the fry of the mouth-breeding cichlid fish, the Mozambique tilapia, for example, hide in their mother's mouth.

A third type of fear is a moment of panic. Overwhelmed with the feeling we are going to die, we have no direction or purpose to our actions. We are so scared we don't know which way to go to save ourselves. We literally run around in circles. All social restraints are lifted; we would kill to live. Here, too, our heart races and our muscles bulge, but we are unable to use our minds to make a plan.

Finally, there is the fear that occurs with a perceived fatal potential, a moment of imminent death. We go into another zone. Time slows down; there is no pain or other sensations. This is seen in animals after a predator has chased them. When touched, they fall to the ground and are immobile. This fear response is called **thanatosis**.[1] Some scientists suggest this may cause the predator to relax his attention and allow the animal another chance to escape. Whether true or not, it is a state of dissociation that allows the animal to avoid the pain of being killed. Each type of fear is associated with a unique neurobiological signature. These signatures are composed of different stress hormones flowing through the brain and body, each aiding a survival response.

Vigilance and salience are required to seek out a predator. The neurochemical dopamine is at the heart of salience. Dopamine increases the signal-to-noise ratio, making things that are salient to an immediate concern stand out against the background. Significant stimuli make their way into our conscious mind, activating centers that say, "Pay attention!" We are now in a vigilant state with another neurochemical on the rise, norepinephrine. Thus, when searching for a predatory threat, a snap of a twig may be all that is necessary to convert salience/vigilance into fight or flight. If the vigilant state was not activated, the snap of the twig may have gone unnoticed.

Flight or fight is all about two chemicals, epinephrine and norepinephrine. Epinephrine (also known as adrenaline) is peripherally secreted by adrenal glands that are located on top of our kidneys. In the same gland are cells that release another chemical critical to survival, **cortisol**. This is not a coincidence, and it reflects, yet again, nature's wisdom. At the same time, norepinephrine (also known as noradrenaline) is released throughout the brain from an area in the brainstem called the **locus coeruleus**. To prepare for a flight-or-fight encounter, epinephrine energizes the body, while norepinephrine does the same for the mind. Many changes occur during this time to improve chances of survival. One of the most dramatic is the decrease in pain sensation, analgesia, associated with norepinephrine. Animals in a battle for survival do not have time to stop and lick their wounds. Boxers take multiple blows that under normal circumstances would hurt. Soldiers can sustain major injuries and continue fighting. This norepinephrine analgesia is critical for survival, and as we shall see, it provides an explanation of chronic pain that can be a consequence of traumatization.

Panic may occur when there is too much norepinephrine. We literally lose all ability to make rational decisions; we cannot see a way out. The planning part of the brain, the prefrontal cortex, is taken offline so all that is left is raw survival actions. The very high levels of norepinephrine shut down the executive planning branch of the brain because it will get in the way of survival. Lifeguards understand that people who are drowning will do anything, including holding them under water, to help stay afloat. No thought, just survival.

The state of dissociation, flaccidity, is about *not* feeling the moment. We are so terrified that sensory input slows down or ceases altogether. Nothing, or at least very little, reaches consciousness. This dissociated state is felt by some researchers to be protective. Thanatosis is about the ultimate dissociation, appearing to be dead. We can't even begin to think about movement. That is what playing dead means.

Types of Fear

Freeze, salience, and vigilance
Fight or flight
Panic
Flaccidity

Fear Is Relayed by Our Senses

The physiological changes produced by fear aid in survival, and fear stimuli need to be simple and readily discernable. The response to these stimuli may be present at birth or develop later. For example, the chicks of the jungle fowl[2] show escape responses to loud noises, but visual escape responses to predators develop later. This makes sense because hearing a strange sound is a less complex task than recognizing a predator. In the duckling, visual patterns are recognized early. These sign stimuli can be responded to, much like noise stimuli, without prior learning (Figure 3.1). Sign stimuli (threatening content) can activate a fear response through any of the senses. For example, a silhouette when moved in one direction over a flock of ducklings induces fear. When moved in the opposite direction it does not. Why should this occur?

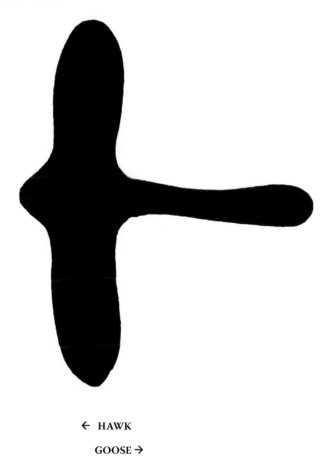

← HAWK

GOOSE →

Figure 3.1 Visual cue stimuli can be innate. (From McFarland, D., *The Oxford Companion to Animal Behavior*, p. 180, Oxford University Press, New York, NY. With permission.)

Flying in one direction, the short neck and long tail are character-istic of a predatory hawk, whereas flying in the other direction, the shadow looks like a goose. Since a rapid fear response is critical to survival, patterns indicating a threat must stimulate action.

Species Have Specific Alarm Systems That Activate Fear

Animals need to avoid predation; fear helps with escape. Reactions must be based on reflex and very simple processing. Alarm responses are of two types: one that internally activates the individual for action, a fight-or-flight response, and one that serves as a warning to other members of its herd. The alarm signals that activate the herd can be visual, auditory, or olfactory. It is the source of the expression "there is safety in numbers," as many eyes are on the alert for predators. For example, pigeons, which usually feed in groups, produce an auditory alarm signal with their wings when they are startled and fly away.[3] This alerts the other pigeons to a potential danger and, in an ever-expanding circle, they take off as well. Auditory alarm calls occur in many species and often have characteristics that make it difficult to locate the calling animal. These calls to other members of the spe-cies produce a "head for cover" or "cover your head" movement. Most are innate, but some are learned. An interesting example of a species-specific auditory alarm call is the yelling of "Fore!" after an errant tee shot. It makes the hearer afraid and reflexively turn away from the sound and cover his or her head.

Olfactory alarms[4] activate the fear response in members of the same species. If a pike fish injures a minnow, the chemicals released from the broken skin keep other minnows away for several hours. These alarm substances most often stimulate flight but can also be used in other ways. The alarm substance of the aggressive slave raider ant not only encourages the members of the colony to fight, but also causes panic in workers of other ant species, making them more vulnerable to attack.

Fear Activates Physiological Changes

A fear response produces a change in our physiology. Our body is put on alert. Increased muscle strength, increased oxygen availability,

Anatomy of the Brain

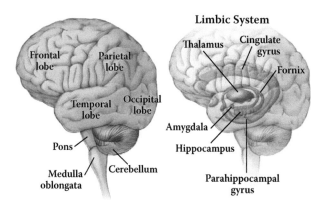

Figure 3.2 Anatomy of the brain. (Medical illustration provided courtesy of Alzheimer's Disease Research, a program of the American Health Assistance Foundation, © 2000–2010, http://www. ahaf.org/alzheimers/)

increased sensory acuity, and the halting of nonsurvival processes such as digestion and grooming are all necessary so we focus only on action. Our mind is put on alert, to try to seek an escape and prepare us to store vital information so that this circumstance can be avoided in the future. From an evolutionary point of view it makes sense that there be one coordinating center. It is called the **amygdala.** Operational at birth (maybe even before), it undergoes changes as the individual matures.[5] The amygdalae are almond-shaped groups of neurons, located on both sides of the brain. Each has its own function. The right amygdala, considered the one in command during fear situations, is located just off the midline, deep inside the temporal lobe. Its location is ideally suited to receive and send information to other areas of the brain (Figure 3.2). It is part of our primitive survival apparatus called the limbic system.

The Limbic System

The limbic system is a construct, loosely defined anatomically, but with a specific function. It is preserved through all mammalian evolution. Its role is to coordinate the activity of various parts of the brain that relate to improving our chances of survival. Some of the anatomical structures assigned to the limbic system include:

Amygdala—involved with emotional expression (fear/rage), memory, and learning.

Hippocampus/Fornix—Involved with learning and storage and retrieval of an event. The fornix connects the hippocampus to the thalamus and hypothalamus.

Thalamus—Receives and sends sensory information and it is modulated by other brain centers.

Cingulate gyrus—Related to orienting to a threatening stimulus and attention.

Hypothalamus—Involved with the release of stress hormones.

Prefrontal cortex—Generally considered an inhibitor of responses arising from the limbic system. Among its functions is threat evaluation.

While the limbic system has many roles, for the purposes of this book it is the ability of this system to encode information vital to survival that is critical. In most mammals, survival is equivalent to escape from a predator. The individual learns not to go where danger lies. In humans, we can survive yet not escape the moment. For example, in a car crash where we are inescapably trapped in the moment. These circumstances produce extreme emotions without a perceived escape. As a consequence and described in detail later, the limbic system inappropriately traumatizes these moments, such that stimuli that recall the moment can reproduce both the emotional and physical experience at the time of the event. In the adult, a functioning limbic system is necessary for traumatization.

In early life, when the limbic system has not completely formed (the hippocampus is not yet functional), highly emotional moments that occur become stored in a separate memory system called procedural memory (see p. 38). This memory system is felt to be located in the dorsal striatum. Although not formally part of the limbic system, it encodes the components of powerful early emotional states via the amygdala[5]. While the cognitive (narrative) component of the event itself is not stored, it affects us nonetheless.

Input Into the Amygdala From Senses

The thalamus receives input from four senses: sight, taste, touch, and hearing (Figure 3.3). Smell, our most primitive sense, has olfactory neurons that bypass the thalamus and head directly to the cortex and, if appropriate, the amygdala. This allows for very rapid, out-of-sight distance evaluation. It is not a good thing to be upwind of a predator. In addition, the thalamus sends its input to the cortex for further processing and, if appropriate, send this processed information to the amygdala.

The right amygdala is a remarkable coordinator for emotional and physiological responses and is made up of a number of areas, called nuclei, each having different functions (Figure 3.4).

Perceived unimodal threatening content (e.g., a loud sound) is directly relayed from the thalamus to the lateral amygdala (LA) as a UFS, signaling danger.

Threatening unimodal content/UFS→Thalamus→LA

In addition to entering the LA, the **unimodal content** also combines with other aspects of the threatening content such as movement, odor, size, shape, and visceral sensation to produce **complex content** that travels from the thalamus to the cortex also entering the LA.

Complex content→Thalamus→Cortex→LA

The sensory stimuli that remain outside the complex content is called the **context**. This travels from the thalamus to the cortex and enters the basolateral amygdala (BLA) via the hippocampus.

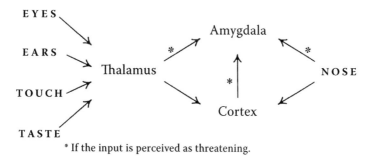

* If the input is perceived as threatening.

Figure 3.3 Pathways from sensory organs to brain areas.

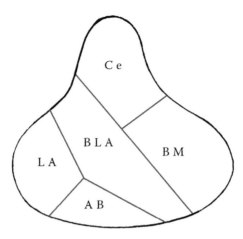

Figure 3.4   Diagram of the amygdala. LA, lateral nucleus; BLA, basolateral nucleus; BM, baso-medial nucleus; Ce, central nucleus; AB, accessory basal nucleus. (Courtesy of Ronald Ruden and Steve Lampasona.)

Sensory Context→Thalamus→Cortex→Hippocampus→BLA

The accessory basal nucleus (AB) is where threatening olfactory content directly enters the amygdala.

Threatening olfactory stimuli→AB

While each area of the amygdala has separate functions, there is much overlap and the neuroanatomy is very similar. For simplicity, these three nuclei, the LA, BLA, and AB, comprise what is called the basolateral complex (BLC).[7] The BLC is where threatening content begin the process of activating action and emotion.

LA/BLA/AB = BLC

Outflow From the Amygdala

The emotional response to a threat is dependent on the BLC activating another part of the amygdala, the central nucleus (CE). The Ce activates and coordinates coordinates the physiological response[8] to sensory input that modulates somatic, endocrine, and autonomic processes. The Ce sends signals to the areas that are involved in fight or flight, danger evaluation, motivation to action, salience and vigilance, orienting, freezing, memory, and pain perception (Table 3.1).[9]

Table 3.1 Outflow From the Central Nucleus

Emotional Stimuli → Thalamus → BLC → Ce → Psychological Responses

BRAIN AREA	RESPONSE
Sympathetic activation	Prepare us for flight or fight
Prefrontal cortex	Aid in danger evaluation
Nucleus accumbens	Motivate us to action
Ventral tegmentum	Increase salience
Locus coeruleus	Increase vigilance
Central grey	Cause freezing
Insula and amygdala	Mediate pain perception

The medial prefrontal cortex (mPFC) as the evaluator of danger is particularly critical for traumatization and has a reciprocal relationship with the amygdala. When the BLC amygdala first perceives fear it inhibits the mPFC, preventing it from shutting down the fear response. This allows the body and mind to prepare for flight or fighting. Under circumstances where evaluation of the threat is made and found not to be significant, the mPFC then sends an inhibitory signal to the amygdala and suppresses the response. Under extreme fear, anger, or chronically stressful conditions this inhibitory signal sent by the mPFC may be reduced and unable to modulate the outflow from the amygdala. This observation suggests a mechanism for **kindling**, a process that predisposes to future traumatization.[10] The BLC also sends information to the hippocampus,[11] a critical structure for encoding and retrieval of the cognitive component. Finally, the BLC is the site where the sensory components of the content (unimodal and complex) and context begin the process leading to their association.

Hardwired Fears: Unconditioned Fear Stimuli (UFS) Directly Enter the Amygdala

What makes input appropriate to be sent to the amygdala? Stimuli that activate the amygdala without prior learning are sensory content called unconditioned fear stimuli (UFS) and are considered innate. These stimuli are recognized and sent directly to the amygdala; no thought is required. Recently, researchers have uncovered a hardwired pathway that produces a fear response.[12] In an experiment, mice placed in a box are stressed and exhibit signs of fear. When this occurs the researchers transfer the air in this box to another box where another mouse is quietly waiting. In the nose of the mouse is a cell called the Gruenberg ganglion that goes directly from the nose to the olfactory alarm system. This cell recognizes alarm odors secreted by frightened mice. In short order, the quiet mouse begins to exhibit signs of fear. In a second set of experiments the researchers cut the connection between the ganglion and the olfactory system in the nonstressed mouse, metaphorically cutting the electrical connection in the mouse's nose. Using conditions identical to the first experiment, the quiet, unstressed mouse fails to respond to the air from the box of the stressed mouse. The conclusions from this study are that mice give off an odor (unimodal sensory content) to warn other mice, but when the neuron containing the receptor for this alarm odor is severed, the warning is not received. This is an example of how nature literally hardwires responses to fear stimuli.

Avoiding Threats to Survival

To avoid predation, action is required. Thought and planning are too slow under most circumstances. Try to catch a fly on the wing and witness astonishing avoidance behavior without thought. In most species, including humans, the brain sends unconditioned (innate, hardwired) fear stimuli directly to the amygdala, alerting us to get out of there. These circuits generate action. No evaluation is necessary. The goal is to avoid the potential predator. We find that a rapidly dropping horizon, or what we call fear of heights (acrophobia), is one of them. Try standing on a rooftop next to the edge. A dropping horizon is one in which we don't know where our leading foot will land or, if we do know, it's not good. A dropping horizon produces fear without assessment. This innate fear of dropping horizon becomes important in understanding certain phobias, such as fear of heights, bridges, ladders, and so on.

Another hardwired fear is that of the dark (nyctophobia). Most mammals have poor night vision. There may be a predator lurking and we can't see it. This is why most horror movies have the scariest scenes in a darkened area. We are hardwired to fear open spaces where there is no place to hide (agoraphobia), and we are hardwired to fear tight spaces (claustrophobia), where we can't escape. Indeed, placing a rat in a tube so that it cannot move is a commonly used stress-inducing procedure in research. We are hardwired to fear loud noises (ligyrophobia), for this suggests a large animal and potential predator. We are hardwired to fear slithery (fear of snakes is called ophidiophobia) and creepy-crawly (fear of insects is called entomophobia) things. We have an emotion called disgust for hardwiring taste and smell. For mammals, there is also the fear of abandonment. This is because mammals are so helpless at birth. Without a mother there is no food or safety; there is only certain death. This is dramatically illustrated in northern mallard ducklings, which, when separated from their mother, will follow a crude duck model, a walking person, or even a cardboard box that is moved slowly away from them. Even as an adult, fear of expulsion from your herd alters behavior, as chances for survival outside the herd are diminished. This powerful fear of abandonment has been used throughout the ages in humans as well. For example, the Catholic Church uses ex-communication and the Amish use shunning to control behavior. Fear of abandonment is one of our primal fears. For humans there are other powerful psychosocial fears that are associated with this, including fear of loss of freedom, social standing, job, and home.

Unconditional (Innate, Hardwired) Fear Stimuli

Abandonment
Being killed
Somatic pain
Heights
Suffocation
Novel situations
Being trapped
Open spaces with no place to hide
Ground-based predators: creepy crawly things
Air-based predators: things out of visual field
Nighttime and darkness
Culture-based fears

This hardwiring does one thing: Once the danger pattern is perceived, it produces a fear response. First and foremost, action must be taken to find a safe place, no questions asked. Evaluation of the threat follows. How do these sensory signals activate the amygdala?

Amygdala Activation

To activate a response from the amygdala, several things must occur. First, the sensing organs need to input the unprocessed sensory information into our brain. This is a process known as transduction, the converting of one thing into another. Thus, the eye, for example, brings into the brain the visual electromagnetic spectrum. Receptors at the back of the eye transduce (convert one form of energy to another) these to electrical impulses along a neuron. After entering and being sorted by the thalamus, when appropriate, threatening stimuli (UFS) are sent to the amygdala for action. They are also sent to the visual sensory cortex where an image is formed and perceived. All sensory input is transduced to electrochemical signals that can be read and interpreted by the brain.

The thalamus acts like a complicated postal service. In addition to sending out information, the thalamus is simultaneously receiving input from other parts of the brain. The cortex sends a signal to the thalamus that increases the salience of a potential threat while diminishing the background noise. Attending to important input is a critical process and requires we minimize distractions. This is why we shut the radio off in our car if we are lost. It allows us to more easily focus on visual stimuli to aid in finding our way. If we need to be extra attentive, a physical component can be added. The external sensory organs help us focus. In the case of the eye, the macula, a dense spot of receptors, is where we focus the image when we want to pay attention. We turn our cupped ear to a sound we want to identify. We taste with the tip of our tongue. In summary, when we seek salience, we must be attentive. This allows us to spot a predator early and activate the amygdala for action. This is vigilance.

When the thalamus senses a hardwired (unconditioned) fear stimulus, it sends it directly to the amygdala for action and creates a fear response. A longer pathway, which handles the more complex aspects of the stimulus (complex content), travels from the thalamus to the cortex to the amygdala and, if appropriate, brings this refined, cortically processed sensory content to an already activated amygdala. Another pathway sends the context (background) to the amygdala via the hippocampus. Input from both sources of processed information can further excite or diminish the amygdala response. These pathways become of critical importance when we explore the mechanisms of traumatization.

If running from a predator is not a viable option, then defensive action must be taken. Fear can be converted into another survival emotion, defensive rage,[13] depending on circumstances. By activating this system, we try to avoid fighting when flight is not possible.

Plan B: Defensive Rage

Frightening a predator away avoids confrontation. Darwin describes the physiognomy of this moment as clenched jaw with the teeth exposed, snarling with an arched back, neck muscles tightened and head held straight, eyes wide and pupils dilated, nasal flaring, expanded chest, and increased height. There is an occasional roar for emphasis. This is defensive rage. This emotion and physiology occurs when fight or flight is not an option: a mother protecting her young from a powerful predator, a child being abused by a much larger adult, a person cornered by a group of thugs. While you will surely lose, the last act before engagement is to produce a moment of defensive rage, hoping to frighten your adversary. Making yourself as big and ferocious and menacing as you can be may make the predator decide not to challenge you. Defensive rage is fear mixed with anger in a situation for which there seems to be no escape (Figure 3.5).

The intruder was about to attack. Slowly she was being backed into the kitchen where she could no longer retreat. Her hands slipped over the top of the sink behind her to see if there was a weapon she could use. She found it, a sharp knife! She grasped it in her hand, arched her back, and lifted the knife blade in the air. Her mouth was clenched, her teeth were bared, and her nostrils were flaring. She stood still, waiting for the intruder to make the first move. Then she would come down on him with the blade.

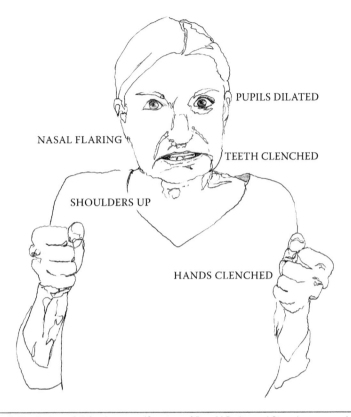

NASAL FLARING

SHOULDERS UP

PUPILS DILATED

TEETH CLENCHED

HANDS CLENCHED

Figure 3.5   Posture of defensive rage. (Courtesy of Ronald Ruden and Steve Lampasona.)

Pathway of Defensive Rage

BLC → Fear → Collateral circumstances → BM → Defensive rage

The expression of rage is driven by collateral circumstances at the time of the event. It is the basal medial nucleus (BM) that appears to be involved with the expression of defensive rage. Rage, like fear, has the potential to be traumatized.

In summary, the LA amygdala detects threat content directly from the thalamus or olfactory bulb in the form of sensory input and activates the amygdala. Subsequently, cortically processed sensory content also enter the LA. Contextual components of the event enter the BLA through the hippocampus (Figure 3.6). The complex content and the context provide for discrimination on whether the threat is real (e.g., is the snake on television, is it in a glass case, or if we are up

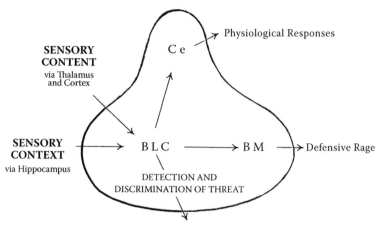

SENSORY CONTENT
via Thalamus and Cortex

C e

Physiological Responses

SENSORY CONTEXT
via Hippocampus

B L C ———→ B M ——→ Defensive Rage

DETECTION AND
DISCRIMINATION OF THREAT

Modulation of All Aspects of Memory Storage
Retrieval and Emotion Generation

Figure 3.6 Flow of information to and through the amygdala. (Courtesy of Ronald Ruden and Steve Lampasona.)

close, is it really a snake or something else). As mentioned earlier, the lateral nucleus, basolateral nucleus (BLA), and the accessory basal nucleus comprise the basolateral complex (BLC).

If the threat is perceived as real, the BLC → Ce output produces a preparatory physiological response that modulates the autonomic and somatic response to the stimulus. As we shall see, it is this modulation of the somatic, autonomic, and emotional components experienced during the event that is critical to explaining the consequences of a traumatization. The BLC modulates the storage and the ability to retrieve the cognitive and emotional components of the event. In certain situations the BLC can also activate the BM, amplifying defensive rage. Under suitable conditions, a flow of information can be ultimately bound together in what we call the traumatic encoding moment. How this binding process[14] occurs is one of the great mysteries of the brain. Suffice it to say that it occurs.

Before we explore the process that encodes this event as a traumatic memory, a further detailed look at how emotions affect memory is given in Chapter 4.

References

1. Wikipedia. *Apparent death.* Retrieved August 17, 2008, from http://en.wikipedia.or/wiki/Apparent_Death
2. McFarland, D. (Ed.). (1982). *The Oxford companion to animal behavior* (pp. 180–181). New York, NY: Oxford University Press.
3. Torrice, M. (2009). *Pigeon wings sound the alarm.* Retrieved from http://sciencenow.sciencemag.org/cgi/content/full/2009/902/2
4. McFarland, D. (Ed). (1982). *The Oxford companion to animal behavior* (pp. 13–14). New York, NY: Oxford University Press.
5. Whalen, J. P., & Phelps, E. A. (2009). *The human amygdala.* New York, NY: Guilford Press.
6. Ferreira, T. L., Shammah-Lagnado, S. J., Bueno, O. F., Moreira, K. M., Fkornari, R. V. & Oliveira, M. G. (2008). The indirect amygdala-dorsal striatum pathway mediated conditioned freezing: insights on emotional memory networks. *Neuroscience* 153(1): 84–94.
7. Rainine, D. G., & Ressler, K. J. (2009). Physiology of the amygdala: Implications for PTSD. In P. J. Shiromani, T. M. Keane, & J. E. LeDoux (Eds.), *Post-traumatic stress disorder: Basic science and clinical practice.* (pp. 39–78). New York, NY: Humana Press.
8. Tanimoto, S., Nakagawa, T., Yamauchi, Y., Minami, M., & Satoh, M. (2003). Differential contributions of the basolateral and central nuclei of the amygdala in the negative affective component of chemical somatic and visceral pains in the rat. *Eur. J. Neurosci.* 18:2343–2350.
9. Akmaev, I. G., Kalmillina, L. B., & Sharipova, L. A. (2004). The central nucleus of the amygdaloid body of the brain: Cytoarchitectonics, neuronal organization, connections. *Neurosci. Behav. Physiol.* 34:603–610.
10. Akirav, I., & Maroun, M. (2007). The role of the medial prefrontal cortex-amygdala circuit in stress effects on the extinction of fear. *Neural Plast.* 2007:30873.
11. Strange, B. A., & Dolan, R. J. (2004). Beta-adrenergic modulation of emotional memory-evoked human and amygdala and hippocampal responses. *Proc. Natl. Acad. Sci.* 101:11454–11458.
    Phelps, E. A. (2004). Human emotion and memory: Interactions of the amygdala and the hippocampal complex. *Curr. Opin. Neurobiol.* 14:198–202.
12. Brechbuhl, J., Klaey, M., & Broillet, M.-C. (2008). Gruenberg ganglion cells mediate alarm pheromone detection. *Science* 321:1092–1095.
13. Shaikh, M. B., & Siegel, A. (1994). Neuroanatomical and neurochemical mechanisms underlying amygdaloid control of defensive rage behavior in the cat. *Braz. J. Med. Biol. Res.* 27:2759–2779.
14. MindPapers. *A bibliography of the philosophy of and science of consciousness.* Retrieved August 18, 2008, from http://consc.net/mindpapers/8.1e. This is a list of papers on the binding problem. Some of these papers can be viewed for free.

4

MEMORY AND EMOTION

To maximize the ability to avoid predation, we need the ability to encode and retrieve fear-producing memories. What are some of the processes ensuring this will occur?

Aside from fleeing and fighting, avoiding similar threatening situations in the future is important for survival. What is needed is a way to store information useful to survival, sustain its clarity, and endow it with a low threshold to recall by similar circumstances. Central to these abilities is the interaction between the amygdala and hippocampus. It is the amygdala's influence on hippocampal-directed encoding and storage of emotional memories that allows them to remain sharp and readily retrievable.

In addition to firsthand experience, we want to be able to encode useful information without necessarily having direct experience. For example, if your mother tells you that a certain place is dangerous, the thought of going there would produce a fear response, and it would probably prevent you from going. By learning without direct experience, we can safely acquire information that is useful for survival. Emotions and thoughts generated by our imagination can thus be encoded. Here, again, the amygdala and hippocampus encode emotional input arising from the mind. They associate and store things we have heard with things we have yet to experience.

The mechanism by which a memory is stored is called consolidation. It is a process that stabilizes a memory trace after the initial acquisition.[1] Consolidation of emotional events is considered to have two distinct phases. Synaptic consolidation, which occurs rapidly, within minutes, involves glutamate receptors, norepinephrine, cortisol, and other chemicals acting in the amygdala and hippocampus. Later, system consolidation occurs as the synaptically consolidated memories become independent of the hippocampus over a period of weeks to years. These memories are stored in the cortex of the brain. (Recently, a third process has become the focus of research—reconsolidation, in which a previously consolidated memory can be made labile again through reactivation of the memory trace.)

During an event that becomes traumatized, the emotional content and the associated sensory and cognitive content become bound into an unforgettable moment. We speculate that *a critical aspect of traumatization is that the unimodal sensory content remains synaptically encoded in the amygdala.* Synaptic encoding of a traumatic event allows us to respond to stimuli recalling the event as if for the first time. The nonthreatening context, however, may undergo further system consolidation.

Memory Systems

Memory storage is divided, more or less, into two separate systems. For a nonemotional event that we can describe by conscious recollection, a narrative, we are using what scientists call the **declarative memory** system.[2] This form of memory is encoded and retrieved via the hippocampus and includes information and factual experiential knowledge. Things we can do but can't describe by narrative are stored in the nondeclarative memory, also known as **procedural memory** system. Procedural memory[3] is the earliest memory system. It is involved with experiencing a feeling with sensory input (e.g., a perfume evokes a certain feeling), skills we learn, habits we acquire, perception of our body's posture, and conditioned responses. It helps us learn how to put food in our mouths, crawl, and speak. It is the location where emotionally intense events [e.g., abandonment or abuse] are stored before the hippocampus is operational at around the age of four. These memories are stored as a "feeling" sense; feelings that occur without cognitive content, such as a sense of safety and comfort or fear and frustration, we experience as an infant. Information stored in either memory system affects our response to subsequent events.

Jon, age 6, born in a refugee camp and adopted at age 15 months, still responded to fire engine sirens, not by covering his ears but with a comforting and defensive wrapping of his arms around his upper body and shivering. Even though he could not recall the sirens of his early childhood, he would exhibit signs of fear.

Emotion-laden events stored in procedural memory via the amygdala are part of what drives our behavior. St. Augustine suggested that while we have the appearance of free will, God predestines our lives. Freud, when he discussed his theories of psychoanalysis, described the role of feelings stored in this manner. He interpreted St. Augustine in a different way. He felt that we do not have free will because we are driven by these subconscious memories. If these memories were traumatized, they never fade. That traumatized memories, stored below conscious awareness and not subject to ready retrieval, are of great consequence is beyond doubt.

The fundamental process required to create a memory is dependent on the neurotransmitter glutamate and its receptors. Glutamate[4] is an excitatory amino acid needed for each new learning and associating process to take place. The mechanism by which glutamate encodes these pathways remains speculative, but it involves the poteniation of post-synaptic glutamate receptors in the amygdala. A traumatic memory can be imagined as neuronal pathways connected by glutamate receptors that are laid down during the event. When reactivated by a stimulus it causes us to reexperience the original moment. This is synaptic consolidation. Interestingly, and this becomes critical in our understanding of the havening process, reactivation of synaptically consolidated glutamate pathways during recall of a traumatic memory appears to make these pathways susceptible to disruption.[5]

There are many neurochemicals involved with this process. One can summarize the actions of these chemicals as follows.

Neurochemicals That Facilitate Storage and Retrieval

Glutamate
Norepinephrine/epinephrine
Acetyl choline
Cortisol
Dopamine

Neurochemicals That Inhibit Storage and Retrieval

GABA
Opioids
Very high cortisol
Serotonin

The Role of Norepinephrine

Most researchers feel that norepinephrine (NE)[6] and cortisol[7] are the key chemicals in the brain that enhance synaptic memory formation associated with emotional events. As mentioned earlier, norepinephrine is released by neurons that originate in the brain stem in an area called the locus coeruleus (LC). The release of NE arises from fear stimuli that activate the Ce. The NE released enters various brain areas.

$$\text{Amygdala}$$

$$\text{Stimulus} \rightarrow \text{BLC} \rightarrow \text{Ce} \rightarrow \text{Locus coeruleus} \rightarrow \uparrow \text{NE} \rightarrow \text{Hippocampus}$$

$$\text{Prefrontal cortex}$$

$$\text{Other brain areas}$$

Norepinephrine enhances learning, and blocking access to its receptor inhibits learning. During an emotionally charged event, markedly increased levels of norepinephrine in the hippocampus, prefrontal cortex, and amygdala, as well as other brain areas, speak to this role. Norepinephrine appears to cause events to form stronger associations, thus making recall easier. This critical role of norepinephrine is not limited to learning, but also plays a part in producing, from content or context, a state of altered physiology, meant to increase our chances for survival. It also plays another role in a circuit that connects the amygdala to the prefrontal cortex.

Norepinephrine in the BLC

Research suggests that when our cortex fully evaluates a threat, and it is found not to be real, an inhibitory signal is sent from the prefrontal cortex to the amygdala. At the onset of activation of the BLC by unconditioned fear stimuli, however, the prefrontal cortex must be prevented from inhibiting amygdala outflow.[8] The release of norepinephrine in the BLC appears to accomplish this. This makes sense from a survival point of view, as we don't want the thinking part of the brain to get in the way when immediate action must be taken.

The Role of Cortisol

Cortisol has been shown to enhance synaptic memory consolidation of emotionally arousing experiences.[7] It is released during stressful circumstances, and all intense emotional states activate the stress response. Cortisol potentiates norepinephrine action and is required for regulating synaptic consolidation in other brain areas.

Very high levels of cortisol released during a traumatizing event appears to affect how the event is stored in memory. These very high cortisol levels produce abnormal hippocampal activity that alters both the storage and subsequent retrieval of an intense emotional event.[9] As a consequence, we cannot consciously recall the event. This is called cognitive dissociation, and the memories are only available in episodic flashbacks, intrusive thoughts, or nightmares. Where and how these memories are stored and retrieved remain uncertain. In general, the inability to consciously recall these dissociated memories is protective; we don't need to actively block the memory from our mind. Unfortunately, this consciously dissociated memory remains biologically active.

What Else Is Needed for Traumatization?

Under nontraumatizing conditions, after experiencing an emotionally charged event, the residual emotional responsiveness on recall of the memory decays over time. On the other hand, after an event is encoded as a traumatic memory, subsequent stimuli can reproduce various aspects of the event as if it were happening for the first time; there is no decrement over time. Special conditions must therefore prevail for an event to be encoded as a traumatization. Chapter 5 explores these conditions.

References

1. Wikipedia. *Memory consolidation.* Retrieved June 2008 from http://en.wikipedia.org/wiki/Memory_Consolidation
2. Wikipedia. *Declarative memory.* Retrieved June 2008 from http://en.wikipedia.org/wiki/Declarative_Memory
3. Tamminga, C. A. (2000). Images in neuroscience. Cognition: Procedural memory. *Am. J. Psychiatry* 157:162. Retrieved from http://ajp.psychiatryonline.org/cgi/reprint/157/2/162.pdf
4. Rainine, D. G., & Ressler, K. J. (2009). Physiology of the amygdala: Implications for PTSD. In P. J. Shiromani, T. M. Keane, & J. E. LeDoux (Eds.), *Post-traumatic stress disorder: Basic science and clinical practice* (pp. 39–78). New York, NY: Humana Press.
   McGaugh, J. L., Roozendal, B., & Okuda, S. (2007). Role of stress hormones and the amygdala in creating lasting memories. In N. Kato, M. Kawata, & R. K. Pitman (Eds.), *PTSD: Brain mechanisms and clinical implications* (pp. 89–103). Japan: Springer Japan.
5. Nader, K., Schafe, G. E., & LeDoux, J. E. (2000). Fear memories require protein synthesis in the amygdala for reconsolidation after retrieval. *Nature* 406:722–726.
6. Roozendaal, B. (2007). Norepinephrine and long-term memory function. In G. A. Ordway, M. A. Schwartz, & A. Frazer (Eds.), *Brain norepinephrine: Neurobiology and therapeutics.* pp. 236–274. Cambridge, UK: Cambridge University Press.
7. Arnsten, A. F. T. (2007). Norepinephrine and cognitive disorders. In G. A. Ordway, M. A. Schwartz, & A. Frazer (Eds.), *Brain norepinephrine: Neurobiology and therapeutics.* pp. 408–435. Cambridge, UK: Cambridge University Press.
8. De Quervain, D. J.-F., Aerni, A., Schelling, G., & Roozendaal, B. (2009). Glucocorticoids and the regulation of memory in health and disease. *Frontiers Neuroendorinol.* 30:358–370.
9. Payne, J. D., Nadel, L., Britton, W. B., & Jacobs, W. J. (2004). The biopsychology of trauma and memory. In D. Reisberg & P. Hertel (Eds.), *Memory and emotion.* New York, NY: Oxford University Press.

ENCODING A TRAUMATIC MEMORY

There are four conditions that need to be met for an event to be encoded as a traumatic memory. First, one needs an emotion-producing event. Second, the event must have meaning for the individual. Third, the brain's neurochemical landscape at the time of the event must be suitable, and fourth, the event must be perceived as inescapable. If these are present, then, through the intermediacy of the amygdala, an enduring imprint of the moment and its associated components is synaptically encoded. The event has been traumatized.

Requirements for Traumatization

Why are some traumatized by an event while others are unscathed? We speculate that there are four conditions that need to be met for a traumatic encoding moment to occur (Figure 5.1).

The Event

Life has traumatic moments. In order for an event to be traumatizing, it must produce an intense emotional response. We can be part of it, we can witness it, or we can be told of it and be traumatized. We can be trapped in a burning building, we can see a building burning and hear the screams of people trapped, or we can hear the stories of burned survivors and be traumatized. A second- or thirdhand account of the event can lead to traumatization because our mind imagines it. This is the origin of vicarious traumatization seen in social workers, therapists, lawyers, police officers, and others dealing with trauma on a regular basis. While a first-person experience will have a greater affect than a third-person account, vicarious traumatization has been studied and workers in the field of trauma therapy must be aware of these dangers.[1]

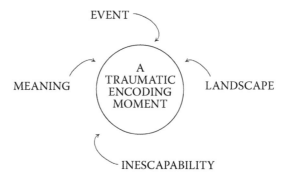

Figure 5.1   Requirements for traumatization. (Courtesy of Ronald Ruden and Steve Lampasona.)

While on an airplane, Samuel experienced severe anxiety when the person in front of him reclined, moving the back of the chair close to his face. He was able to trace this back to a moment when his mother told him that she did not want to be buried underground. He had imagined his mother in a coffin, with the lid close to her face, and this traumatized him. This vicarious traumatization overlapped with the feeling of being trapped on the plane and initiated an anxiety response.

The event does not have to be life threatening or even put us at risk. Riding down an escalator hardly qualifies as a dangerous activity, yet this event strikes fear in those with a fear of heights. Swimming in water over your head (drowning/suffocation) can be fear producing. Watching an animal killed can frighten you (vicarious). Seeing your child sick can be frightening (loss/abandonment). Even made-up stories with horrible endings can produce fear (imaginary). The list of things that can produce strong emotions is endless.

In the final analysis, the emotional event must cause norepinephrine and cortisol to rise to high levels to meet this requirement for traumatization. Norepinephrine prepares our mind for quick action and increases our ability to process, associate, and store information. Norepinephrine also activates an amygdala-prefrontal pathway, preventing the prefrontal cortex from inhibiting the amygdala. Cortisol enhances norepinephrine's actions. Dopamine is also elevated at this time, causing the content and context of the event to become more salient.

Meaning

The second requirement for traumatization is that the event has meaning to the individual. Meaning arises as a result of our innate need for attachment and our previous experiences. Meaning is understood early on when, as an infant, we see our mother walk into the room and we smell her skin, knowing that we will be held and caressed. We will also have our wet diaper changed, and the uncomfortable sensation of hunger will evaporate when we get to drink the milk she provides. Her entrance is all about pleasure and the removal of pain. The meaning of this entrance obviously changes over time, but it is arguably the most powerful attachment we will ever experience.

We are, of course, highly attached to living, and the potential loss of our life is certainly meaningful. Indeed, the possibility of being killed produces an intense emotional response. A traumatizing event, however, does not always involve a life-or-death moment. Any loss of attachment can cause great emotional turmoil. The loss of stature in your community, the loss of youth, the loss of self-esteem, the loss of ability to provide for your family, the loss of a limb, even the loss of a tooth are all meaningful events. Whether this loss leads to a traumatization depends on the other requirements being met.

Meaning is not just about self. Loss of any attachment, such as your child, spouse, parent, friend, caregiver, lover, pet, or country, is filled with meaning. Attachment, the not being alone, drives us to form friendships, exhibit patriotism, join country clubs and houses of worship, and live in certain communities. The armed forces develop this meaning to produce cohesive units, ready to sacrifice for those to whom you have become attached. It is this fear of loss of attachment that gives power to meaning.

We can also have attachments to nonliving things. Our home is a place of great meaning. It is full of memories to which we are attached. Losing our home because of natural events (flood, fire, and all that nature can produce) or financial events (loss of job, becoming disabled) or man-made events (war, loss of a sense of safety) can be traumatizing. For example, loss of a sense of security in our home, if it is burglarized, can be traumatizing.

Buddha recognized attachments as the cause of craving and suffering. He strove to rid himself of these attachments by becoming one with the universe.[2] Most of us are unable to accomplish this and our attachments cause suffering. It is often only through the pain we experience when an attachment is lost—through death, separation, or a simple breakup—that we begin to appreciate its power. It is from this feeling we learn to protect that to which we are attached.

Aside from the emotional needs, attachment also has a physical component: touch. There is a powerful biological need for mammals to be held, caressed, comforted, and cuddled. Touch is how Michelangelo's God gives life to Adam in the Sistine Chapel. Touch has an extrasensory component that provides meaning. It is what drives animals to herd. As Francis Galton,[3] the 19th century naturalist, observed:

> The ox ... cannot endure even a momentary severance from its herd. If he be separated from it by stratagem or force, he exhibits every sign of mental agony; he strives with all his might to get back again and when he succeeds, he plunges into its middle, to bathe his whole body with the comfort of close companionship.

Attachments, physical, personal, and public, are the fundamental brick and mortar of meaning. Without attachment there is no meaning.

Meaning can also be based in previous experience. Events that in and of themselves may not appear to be threatening to observers can be a reminder of terrifying events from another's past. Thus, Susan, who had been kidnapped and molested when she was a youngster, screamed and cried hysterically when a stranger unexpectedly patted her on the behind. It was this earlier event that gave meaning to a seemingly minor incident. While events that evoke intense feelings in most individuals are easy to recognize, one's past, flush with meaning for the individual, may be all that is needed to produce a traumatization. It is therefore not for us to judge what constitutes a meaningful event. Thus, in searching for the traumatizing event, do not dismiss clues that may seem trivial to you.

Landscape Needed for Traumatization

What is a landscape? One can define the landscape of the brain as its neurochemical state at any given time. For the purposes of this model we have chosen five neurochemicals believed to be necessary for traumatization (there are, of course, other molecules, such as acetyl choline, involved). These substances are glutamate, dopamine, serotonin, norepinephrine, and cortisol, and they affect how information is processed in the brain. As baseline (tonic release), these chemicals act as **neuromodulators** affecting mood, information processing, and altering our vulnerability to traumatization.

During acute stress, the levels of these regulatory neurochemicals are dramatically increased (phasic release). These higher levels cause information to be processed differently and are necessary for traumatization. It is here they act as **neurotransmitters**, telling the body to get ready. These new levels make us pay attention, sharpen our senses, motivate us to action, and prepare the brain to store the incoming sensory information. Thus, rising dopamine will occur when we are seeking the presence of a potential predator, as it increases our ability to recognize predator-related cues. When fighting or fleeing, high norepinephrine and epinephrine prepare our mind and body. Serotonin also rises slightly to prevent the system from becoming overwhelmed. Glutamate is involved with all of these processes.

These neurochemicals are also altered during chronic inescapable stress. Here, tonic levels of serotonin appear to be lower, and depending on the circumstances, cortisol and norepinephrine can be either elevated or decreased. Chronic stress appears to alter the landscape of the brain in such a way as to make it more vulnerable to traumatization. This is why traumatization (a form of inescapable stress) begets further traumatization.

Neuromodulators and Neurotransmitters

A neuromodulator is a substance that affects information processing and is secreted at a homeostatic baseline level. The baseline levels of neuromodulators reflect the sum of our inherent psychological makeup, old traumas, internal physiological states, recent experiences, and hormone levels. Neurotransmitter release is predicated on the perception of a threatening or novel stimulus. The brain is made of various interacting subsystems, each with its own types of neurochemical receptors. These receptors can activate protein synthesis or alter the permeability of the neuron to which it is attached. The release of these neurochemicals can produce short-term action or long-time change. The neurochemicals involved with traumatization act both as modulators and transmitters.

> *Norepinephrine—As a neuromodulator it regulates mood and anxiety. It provides for greater accuracy in retrieval of information. As a neurotransmitter it activates our physiology needed for fleeing or fighting, increases our vigilance, and improves our ability to store and retrieve information and produce analgesia. Norepinephrine is essential to inhibit the outflow from the prefrontal cortex to the amygdala, thereby shifting control over behavior to the amygdala.*

> *Dopamine—As a neuromodulator it sets the stage for alertness and smooth movement, helping us seek out what is important and go there or run from it. As a neurotransmitter it is used to increase salience, vigilance, and motivate action.*

> *Serotonin—As a neuromodulator, elevated levels decrease one's ability to seek related information and provide resilience to traumatization. Serotonin prevents us from becoming overwhelmed by too much sensory input. Conversely, lower levels increase our ability to form associative connections and increase susceptibility to traumatization. Behaviorally, lower tonic levels are associated with aggressive and compulsive activity. As a neurotransmitter, elevated levels of serotonin, along with other neurochemicals, provide for a feeling of satiety and safety.*

> *Cortisol—As a neuromodulator it regulates many systems (e.g., immune) in the body and has a known diurnal rhythm. Released during stress, it appears necessary for encoding and healing.*

Glutamate—An excitatory amino acid (EAA) neurotransmit-
ter that also increases the effect of other neurochemicals. It is
critical for storage and retrieval and for linking components of
an event. Without glutamate and its receptors, no information
will be stored. Glutamate and its receptors light the pathway by
which information travels.

GABA—An inhibitory amino acid (IAA) neurotransmitter that
acts by promoting the effect of other neurochemicals. Through its
action storage and retrieval of information are inhibited. It is yin
to glutamate's yang. If glutamate opens a path, GABA closes it.

A Vulnerable Landscape

As mentioned above, the levels of these neurochemicals are modulated
by our inherent sensitivity to stressors, our inherent psychological
makeup (temperament, compulsive tendencies, etc.), environmental
influences (living conditions, puberty), recent experiences, and long-
term memories that include earlier traumatic memories.

What are some of the circumstances that alter these levels and
increase our vulnerability to traumatization? Recent research has
shown that adverse prenatal and early postnatal experiences can influence long-term development (see www.developingchild.net). Puberty
is one of the great landscapers of the brain. This landscaping is due
largely to the effects of testosterone and estrogen on the brain. These
substances act as physiological stressors of enormous power, as shown
by the intense effect these substances have on rational thought and
emotional behavior.

The role of previous experiences on susceptibility to traumatization
is critical. As mentioned earlier, the term used in psychiatry is kindling,
which means previous stressful events can alter sensitivity to future
events. On a molecular level, kindling produces an increase in excitatory glutamate transmission and a decrease in inhibitory GABA transmission in the amygdala. Prior stressful events change perception for a
current event. For example, preschoolers who witnessed the September
11 attack on the World Trade Center were at high risk for developing
lingering emotional and behavioral problems only if they had had a
previous frightening experience, like seeing a parent fall ill. It is unclear

from this study whether these earlier frightening experiences resulted in traumatization. Nonetheless, it was found that 40% of those who had such sequential traumas suffered from depression, emotional outbursts, and poor sleep three years later. By contrast, children who saw the attack or its victims but had no such earlier trauma showed few, if any, psychological scars. What is remarkable is that previous traumatic events could be anything from a dog bite to a serious accident.[4] This simple but powerful illustration broadens our understanding about what can sensitize an individual to traumatization. How does anyone get through life without one of these seemingly minor experiences that can kindle? And if so, why doesn't everyone become traumatized?

What clinical features guide us to know who is more susceptible? Vulnerability is increased by overly empathetic abilities, low self-esteem, and difficulty in regulating the level of emotional response. Personality traits such as obsessive-compulsive disorders, anxiety, introversion, and substance abuse also increase risk. The stressors caused by poverty and low education levels independently increase risk for traumatization.

A Resilient Landscape

Resilience to traumatization, on the other hand, is associated with good intellectual functioning, the ability to regulate emotional responsiveness, optimism, appropriate attachment behaviors, an active problem-solving approach to circumstances, and a sense of being self-contained, that is, experiencing moderate needs and desires. One can also landscape the brain to aid in resilience. Techniques such as yoga, meditation, and exercise can improve our chances of avoiding traumatization (see Appendix B).

Inescapability

Escape requires movement and fear can produce it. Running, jumping, climbing, flying, burrowing, swimming, and fighting all involve motion. If we cannot move or hide we are trapped. A perceived inescapable threatening situation has the potential to traumatize. The perception need not last long, nor is it necessary for this perception to reach conscious awareness. Inescapability can occur during a car accident, when you are falling down, when you cross a bridge, when you are in a combat situation, or when you are told you have cancer. There are many life events for which there is no place to run and hide. It is that moment when the thinking and planning part of the brain, the prefrontal cortex, is taken offline and we are subject to control by amygdala outflow. When all four requirements are met, the event is encoded as a traumatization.

I am a 48-year-old widow who lost my 41-year-old husband of 22½ years in a very tragic accident on January 5, 2006. We had a wonderful marriage and family life; we had one beautiful child and were very much in love. Larry* was my soul mate. He was an absolutely wonderful man; everyone I knew loved him. He was an amazing dad to our child, and his loss has just about ruined her as well. What happened? It was the day after Christmas 2005, he was on vacation until January, and he woke up one morning and said, "Who wants to go on a random road trip to Florida?" My daughter and I replied, "We do. We do." And within hours our minivan was packed, headed to Florida. We spent an amazing 10 days there; I must say the last 10 days of his life were amazing! On our drive back to Massachusetts, I reached over to him and said, "Kiss me, I love you so much and hope I die before you, because I don't think I could ever live without you." And he replied, "Don't worry, Hon, I am going to die before you, I am going to die young."

The very next day he went to work, called me around 10:30 a.m. just to tell me that he missed me, what he wanted for dinner, and said he would call before leaving so I could boil the water for the ravioli I was making. He called me every day when he left work. So he called me, said there was a problem and he would be a little late (he was the building engineer for a commercial real estate company in Boston). I then received a phone call two hours later saying he would be later, as something else had come up. (That was the last contact he had with anyone according to the cell phone record.) Immediately after the phone call, I had a very strange feeling inside; I then proceeded to call him over and over again, no answer. A few times I had a fleeting thought that something was wrong, but didn't act on it—I just assumed he was very busy. Three hours later my phone rang and all the man said was, "Mrs. Stanger, this is the president of Hopewell Industries [that's where he worked]." And I screamed, "Larry is dead!" I just knew it. He said, "No, but there has been

---

* Story used with permission; identities changed to protect confidentiality.

*a terrible accident and you need to get to Cambridge Hospital right away."
There are no words to express the sheer terror that came into my body all of a
sudden. I forgot how to get to the highway, just a few minutes from my house;
what should have taken 20 minutes took an hour and a half. My daughter's
boyfriend drove us. When we did get there, a policeman escorted Lilly (our
daughter) and me into a small room. The doctor just turned his head (I will
never forget that image) and shook it. He told me he was gone. I screamed "No,
no, no!" for a few minutes, and suddenly felt as though it was all a dream.*

*Larry had been up on the roof, 4½ stories high; he was looking at a vent
shaft and slipped off the roof. On his fall down he took out a huge window
air conditioner and probably bled to death because, although people heard a
loud crash, nobody went out until 45 minutes later.*

*The next few months were surreal. Many times I felt as though it was
all a bad dream and that I would eventually wake up and tell him what
happened. But, of course, that never happened. What made it extremely
difficult was how he died—that made the grief much more complicated.
Fortunately, I met a woman at the church who gave me a beautiful thought;
she said that as Larry was falling, the angels were caressing him and he did
not feel a thing. That thought has brought me much comfort.*

*Prior to this horrific tragedy, I never had any emotional issues. I always
felt that I had a very strong, balanced mind and a wonderful outlook on
life; never believed in medication of any sort—both Larry and I always
felt society was overmedicated. We were very spiritual and basically very
content. We tended to view the world from the same set of eyes. When it
first happened, I did call my primary care doctor for something to help me
sleep, because I was racing so much. I could go three to four days without
sleep; it was horrible. I believe I grieved rather well, if there is such a
thing. I cried, sobbed, cried, and sobbed for months and months. About the
third week after the accident, I had a wonderful dream where he called
me and said "Hi" in a very happy tone, the way he would say hi when he
called our daughter, and he said, "I'm OK." And I screamed, "Larry, are
you in heaven?"*

*And he chuckled in this very happy tone and said, "Yes, I am." When I
woke up, it was the strangest thing, I had this sort of buzzing vibration
in my left ear, and I felt so wonderful (a feeling that lasted a few weeks),
because it was so important for me to know he was okay. The months went
on. My daughter and I did not grieve together; she went to live with her*

new boyfriend and I became suicidal and depressed. As time went on I began trying everything to move past the darkness. I ran several miles a day, went to the gym, and started practicing martial arts. I constantly felt I was racing and running, and I guess in a sense I was: I was running from my pain. All in all, I would say I did very well with my grief, as I feel my strong spiritual foundation helped me. Although, in the course of the grief, I did feel anger at God, but thankfully that has passed. I now realize we each come to this life experience with a purpose, and a job, and when it is done, we return to the spirit world.

About 10 months after his death, a distant relative passed away at 39 years old; she had lupus. She had been with her husband about the same amount of time I had been with mine, and they had a similar soul mate relationship. I initially reached out to him because I didn't want him to go to the hellish dark places I did, as I felt I did a good job in preventing that for myself. They had a little son who at the time was almost 6, and he was very sickly. He was born a twin and a preemie and spent his first year of life in the hospital. When I met the little boy he was on a feeding tube and in diapers and only spoke in one- or two-word utterances. After four months of my being in his life, I got him off the feeding tube and potty trained. I took him to specialists and found out he was severely autistic, and now, three years later, he has been diagnosed with epilepsy, mental retardation, ADHD, a periventricular brain injury, and a white matter brain disease of unknown etiology. This little boy was like my medicine—all the love I had for Larry I was able to pour into him and into my helping him. So, they came to live with us and life became very challenging (this was about a year after Larry's death). I believe this is when the PTSD started to kick in.

I couldn't concentrate, became very agitated at things that would never bother me. I couldn't tolerate sitting in traffic, waiting in lines, stress from Junior (the little boy). I had broken sleep, couldn't fall asleep, or if I did, I would awaken every few hours feeling very racy (this still happens). Whenever Lilly would go out (which is not often), I would panic if I heard fire engines or ambulances. I envisioned her in an accident and became terrified, like crazy, and would feel all the physical symptoms I did that night in the hospital when Larry died. I get very thirsty, I have to go to the bathroom, and just shake and become filled with immense fear. When she goes out I text her and call her several times to be sure she is okay, and this is so unhealthy for her as well as myself, as I feel it is destroying my insides. I was always a peaceful, patient person, and now I have no peace and am extremely impatient, especially while driving. I get so infuriated at the most trivial things. I cannot concentrate (I almost feel as though I have ADD now). I feel like one huge ball of anger, and this is not me—not who I ever was. I just want to feel at peace again. It is ruining my relationships, my life, my daughter's, and Arnold and his son, who live with me. I really need help. I just want to get better.

As far as treatment and meds go, they did give me the lowest dose of lorazepam (an antianxiety medication) when the accident happened to help me with sleep. I take them when I cannot sleep, or if I am in a panic when Lilly goes out and I cannot contact her. I also tried grief therapists in the beginning, but fired them all, as I realized there was nothing any of them could do for me. I felt it was a spiritual thing that I had to go through myself, and I feel as far as the grief went, I did grieve in a very healthy way. Then I found the Trauma Center just outside of Boston. I was seeing a therapist there and she tested me and said I had depression and PTSD. I was, and still am, extremely hypervigilant—no intrusions thankfully; they subsided early on. Since I was against meds, my therapist suggested I try St.-John's-wort, which did help with giving me energy to do things, clean my house, and cook again, but it did nothing for the panic and the PTSD. She also gave me EMDR, which seemed like it was helping. We never got to the point of going through the entire treatment. It started to get very expensive, and then I got angry because she said she couldn't treat my daughter, as it would be a conflict of interest. So the old ugly PTSD reared itself and I fired her. I then asked my primary care doctor for meds, as it's gotten so bad. I just want this PTSD out of my life. I tried sertraline (an antidepressant, antianxiety medication) for about six days, and after taking it I would start to get anxious and had to take lorazepam to calm down. I did not like the feeling, so I stopped it. I then tried citralopram (another antidepressant/antianxiety medication) and it did the same thing, so I am on nothing now.

All I want is to heal, to be calm again, and to be able to clean my house, cook, take care of my gardens, and help my daughter. I do have plans to write a handbook on sudden traumatic death, as there is really nothing out there (at least not written by someone who experienced it and survived it). But there is no way I can do this, as my ability to concentrate is gone. I am definitely a warrior, but this is one battle I cannot seem to fight on my own.

Her experience certainly produced an intense emotional response and it is likely this resulted in traumatization. However, it was the subsequent stress arising from the challenges of caring for an autistic child that altered her landscape allowing for the production of symptoms and a diagnosis of PTSD. When you finish Chapter 8, come back to this story and try to see what moments you would choose to haven. Chapter 10, on trauma cures, recounts what happened to her after havening.

Traumatization

A memory is traumatically encoded when the brain is vulnerable and escape from an emotion-generating event is not perceived to be possible. While some of the processes leading to this type of encoding are known, much remains a mystery. The only good thing about this mystery is that we know where to look for answers—in the brain. Unfortunately, the brain is still a bigger mystery, and here we heap a mystery upon a mystery. What sounds like a fruitless search is not. We are now able to map the brain using various techniques. We can use chemical probes, scanning techniques, and lesional (destroying part of the brain in laboratory animals) and clinical methods to dissect the neural happenings. It is from the knowledge harvested from research that we begin to understand this process.[5]

To be able to erase a traumatically encoded memory, we must first have a common language with which to speak. We define traumatization at the neural level *as the process that permanently encodes and synaptically consolidates linkages between the emotional, cognitive, autonomic, and somatosensory components present during the traumatizing event. Any one of the components recalled either consciously or subconsciously, activates the amygdala and causes the release of stress neurochemicals. For each reactivation, we experience some or all of the components as if they were happening for the first time.*

It is important to note that these components are stored in several places in the brain. It is the amygdala that modulates the binding of the components present during the traumatizing event. Further explanations are required. When we use the word emotional, we are referring to the affective response to an event. Emotion is a felt sense. By cognitive we mean both the content and the context of the event. In recalling a traumatic moment, the context is often overshadowed by the fear stimulus and is not readily retrievable. By autonomic we mean the automatic brain functions that help us swallow, regulate body temperature, speak fluently, and control waste disposal. By **somatosensory** we mean sensed throughout our bodies, such as pain, numbness, tingling, skin temperature, hypersensitivity to touch, and other sensations.

Components of a Traumatic Memory

Emotional
Autonomic
Cognitive—Both conscious and subconscious components
Somatosensory

By **subconscious** we mean mental content, generated by internal or external cues, not consciously registered, but nonetheless able to stimulate somatic symptoms and emotional arousal. **Conscious** means mental content we hold in thought or attention and we are aware of its presence and meaning.

We specifically avoid here the ambiguity of what makes an event traumatic. Since not everyone who experiences the same event is traumatized, an operational definition that defines the process and consequences of encoding is preferred.

The cognitive component of the memory of the traumatized event accessible to conscious retrieval is simply called a **traumatic memory**. These memories are bound into a coherent narrative whole. The cognitive and emotional response are linked. Cognitively **dissociated traumatic memories** are stored and/or retrieved differently. They are brought to conscious awareness without effort or control on our part through flashbacks, nightmares, intrusive thoughts, and bodily sensations.

> *Traumatic memory—Thoughts and emotions that are associated with conscious activation or inadvertent reminders that lead to recalling of the event and its emotional content. Stress-related neurochemicals are released.*

> *Dissociated traumatic memories—Thoughts, feelings, and sensations that are experienced when activated by stimuli that arise from abnormal retrieval and cause the release of stress neurochemicals.*

Dissociated Traumatic Memories

Dissociation is a complex and poorly understood phenomenon.[6,7] Parts of a traumatic event can be dissociated and remain beyond conscious recall. This type of memory is puzzling because when it enters consciousness, the individual cannot relate it to his or her current state. Emotions may appear unbidden. Pain may be present but the cause is a mystery. All sorts of autonomic dysfunction may occur.

Beth had severe localized chest pain and tenderness. There was no evidence of any recent trauma. Her life was about to change because her husband had been convicted of a crime and was about to be jailed. She was terrified that she could not provide for her children. The last time she felt this fear was when she had a lung biopsy at the site of the current pain. This also produced terror, when she was afraid she might have cancer and would die and not be able to provide for her children.

Here a similar emotional feeling, the fear of not being able to care for her children, brought out a somatic component.

To make matters even more complicated, dissociation may not be just the result of an extremely horrific moment where very high cortisol levels disrupt hippocampal functioning. Dissociation may also be developmental. If traumatizing events occurred in early childhood, generally before the age of 4, the cognitive portion of the event cannot be stored because the hippocampus, the narrative memory processing center, has not yet developed. The emotional components, however, remain biologically active. Thus, early childhood traumatization, such as abandonment or physical or emotional abuse, may cause permanent alteration of the landscape by continual activation of stress neurochemicals.

Regardless of whether the amygdala is activated by memories we actively recall or by stimuli that remain subconscious, the consequences of a traumatization remain the same: Intermittent or persistent activation by a component of a traumatic memory causes the release of stress neurochemicals and the experience of other components. The neurobiological response to the chronic release of stress chemicals soon becomes maladaptive, landscaping the brain to produce strange behavior, strange thinking, and disease and increase vulnerability to further traumatization.

Sensory Input and Emotion

How does the sensory information about the event get to the amygdala to produce an emotional response and set the stage for traumatization? There are two ways: One is directly from the thalamus. The other way is via the cortical structures after processing.[8] All sensory information (except olfactory) arrives at the thalamus unprocessed. As mentioned earlier, certain survival-based stimuli (UFS) (e.g., heights) produce a fear response without further processing. These unconditioned fear stimuli are hardwired, innately recognized as threatening and flow from the thalamus directly to the amygdala for action. It is the way we are able to rapidly respond when there is a stimulus that is perceived as danger. Norepinephrine and cortisol are immediately released.

This thalamic → amygdala pathway produces the emotional core. If an event is traumatized, the focus of unimodal sensory input (e.g., a gun, bridge, face, etc.) that associates with the UFS also activates the amygdala.

Other, more complex sensory information, such as size, speed, color, shape, pain, visceral sensations, and sounds of the fear-producing stimulus, enters the thalamus and is sent to various parts of the brain (visual cortex for sensory information entering through the eyes, auditory cortex for the ears, and so on), processed, and if appropriate, enters the amygdala via the lateral nucleus (LA). This processed information travels via the cortical route (the long route) arriving at the amygdala milliseconds after the unprocessed thalamic input. The background context goes by the long route and enters an activated BLA via the hippocampus (Figure 5.2).

This is of critical importance for traumatization (see below). Once the amygdala is activated via the short path by sensory input associated with a hardwired fear stimulus (UFS), complex content and context, having taken the long route, now enter an activated amygdala. This

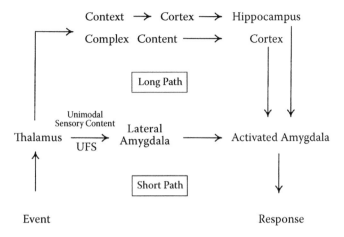

Figure 5.2   The short path activates the amygdala, which is now receptive to cortically processed information. (Adapted from LeDoux, J. E. 1994. Associations, memory, and the brain. *Scientific American* 270: 50–51.)

processed input encounters an amygdala with an elevated norepinephrine and cortisol level and an activated memory trace mediated by a specific glutamate receptor pathway for the UFS. If encoded as a traumatization, these complex content and context then become bound to the emotional core of the event.

Modulation of Response to an Emotional but Nontraumatizing Event

Imagine you are walking in the woods and see something move on the ground. This activates the amygdala and you jump back, prepared for action. This activated basolateral complex (BLC) sends a signal to the Ce and an inhibitory signal to the medial prefrontal cortex (mPFC), allowing full amygdala outflow. In a very short time, perhaps milliseconds, your cortically processed information recognizes the movement as a stick (complex content). You calm down because the object is no longer viewed as a threat. Alternatively, if the object is a snake and you become frightened but feel you are at a safe distance (context), you will also calm down. Perception of safety inhibits the outflow from the Ce via GABA neurons activated by a signal from the mPFC (Figure 5.3).

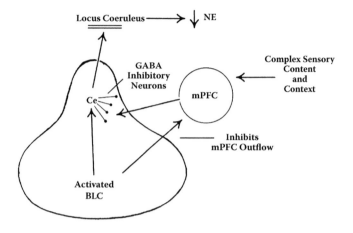

Figure 5.3 First, BLC inhibits mPFC, and if safety is perceived (via complex sensory content or context), mPFC inhibits Ce → //LC → ↓NE. (Adapted from Quirk, G. J. et al. 2003. Stimulation of medial prefrontal cortex decreases the responsiveness of central amygdala output neurons. *J. Neurosci.* 23: 8000–8807.)

Thus, for a short time, emotions rule over the evaluative part of the brain. However, if the evaluation does not reveal a threat or you feel safe, reason prevails, you calm down, and a potentially traumatizing moment is avoided.[9]

The Traumatization of an Event

We have described the requirements for traumatization and the components of a traumatic memory. We have discussed the roles of the BLC and hippocampus in associating the components of a traumatic event, and the Ce in activating the requisite physiology, the actions of neurotransmitter chemicals such as glutamate, norepinephrine, and cortisol, and the importance of the mPFC. In the event where there is no perceived escape, a pathway lit by glutamate receptors, leading to all components of the traumatizing moment is permanently encoded:

Mechanism of Traumatization

Stimulus [unimodal and UFS] pass through thalamus → Signal to amygdala → Fear/defensive rage generated → ↑NE and cortisol in

amygdala → Inhibition of mPFC → Complex content and context enter amygdala → Four requirements met → Glutamate receptors in BLC amygdala potentiated → BLC modulates binding of the components of event → A traumatic memory is stored

The Timing of Traumatization

When during an emotional event does the encoding occur? Clinical evidence suggests that it occurs during the moment of flight or fight, when escape is perceived not to be possible or fighting is futile. It is this moment where the stress neurochemicals norepinephrine, dopamine, and cortisol are elevated. Traumatization is a high norepinephrine and dopamine landscape, clear, focused, and in the moment.

References

1. Adams, S. A., & Riggi, S. A. (2008). An exploratory study of vicarious trauma among therapist trainees. *Training Educ. Prof. Psychol.* 2:26–34. Retrieved from http://www.apa.org/apags/profdev/victrauma.html
2. O'Brien, B. *Why do Buddhists avoid attachment? Attachment may not mean what you think it means.* Retrieved January 30, 2010, from http://buddhism.about.com/od/basicbuddhistteachings/a/attachment.htm
3. Galton, F. (1883). *Inquiries into human faculty and its development* (p. 49). Retrieved from http://galton.org/books/human-faculty/text/html/galton-1883-human-faculty2.html
4. Chemtob, C. M., Nomura, Y., & Abramovitz, R. A. (2008). Impact of conjoined exposure to the World Trade Center attacks and to other traumatic events on the behavioral problems of preschool children. *Arch. Pediatr. Adolesc. Med.* 162:126–133.
5. LeDoux, J. E. (1996). *The emotional brain. The mysterious underpinnings of emotional life.* New York, NY: Simon & Shuster.
6. Van der Kolk, B. A., & Fisler, R. (1995). *Dissociation and the fragmentary nature of traumatic memories: Overview and exploratory studies.* Retrieved from http://www.trauma-pages.com/vanderk2.htm
7. Vermetten, E., Dorahy, M. J., & Spiegel, D. (Eds.). (2007). *Traumatic dissociation: Neurobiology and treatment.* Washington, DC: American Psychiatric Publishing.
8. LeDoux, J. E. (1994). Emotion, memory and the brain. *Sci. Am.* 279:50–57.
9. Quirk, G. J., Likhtik, E., Pelletier, J. G., & Pare, D. (2003). Stimulation of medial prefrontal cortex decreases the responsiveness of central amygdala output neurons. *J. Neurosci.* 23:8800–8807.

6

CAUSES AND CONSEQUENCES
OF TRAUMATIZATION

What common circumstances create a landscape permissive for traumatization? It is worthwhile to explore some of these sources, as this will be helpful in leading us to certain core emotional issues that need to be explored if we are to attempt to treat the consequences of traumatization.

Early Events

The Causes We All Share
Trauma of birth
Fear of suffocation
Fear of abandonment
Hunger

Birth is traumatic. Here we were, for many months, in a warm, relaxing sea, being fed, housed, and comforted by the sounds of our mother's heartbeat. We think of attachment as something that is postnatal, but the most critical attachment of our life occurs when the fertilized egg attaches to the mother's womb. This is the primary attachment, and from the comfortable, fully grown fetus's point of view, birth is an unrequested detachment. During labor we are pushed against an opening way too small, and pushed and pushed. This is painful and physiologically arousing for both mother and soon-to-be newborn. Such arousal is necessary because the next few moments are critical.

As a result of the mother's labor, we are literally squeezed out into a strange world, bereft of the most life-sustaining element, oxygen. We rapidly starve for air and, in the most life-affirming moment, we gasp our first breath. The fear of suffocation is avoided. Then we cry out. This is not an ordinary cry: This is a cry for survival. It is resonant and full lunged, demanding attention and compelling action. The mother's brain has also been signaled during labor. During this time, oxytocin, a maternal bonding hormone, is released in huge quantities into the mother's brain. (Note: In nature's efficiency, oxytocin also causes the uterus to contract to aid in expelling the fetus.) The baby's cry compels the mother to hold the baby. The reunion of mother and baby, the simple touch, and the calming stroking by the mother quiet both, and the trauma of abandonment is avoided.

Finally, the food that the mother's placenta had so generously provided is no longer available. The newborn becomes very hungry as its rapidly growing body demands to be fed. While not imminent, starvation is at stake. At this moment the newborn has only one call for help and it cries. This has worked before to prevent abandonment. This cry has a remarkable effect and milk pours into the mother's breast, causing her pain. We continue to wail until the nipple is in the mouth and food and touch are provided. Nature's wisdom is seen here; the reunion removes both mother and child's pain.

At birth, these sources almost never produce a traumatization. If any one of these events failed to occur, the child died. However, extra ordinary stress (e.g., difficult forceps delivery), may be encoded in procedural memory via an activated amygdala. If encoded as a trauma, it may act as a neuromodulatory landscaper. In the 1950s, hospitalized children were severely restricted from seeing their parents for fear that an infection may be transmitted. These children felt frightened and abandoned. Upon returning home their behavior was disturbed. As reported by a mother:

> I left John (twenty-one months old), on admittance, happily playing about the ward, quite fearless in his relationship with the nurse and other children. He came home with no confidence at all. He would not go to his daddy and I could not leave him at all, because he screamed and sobbed. He was frightened of being touched by me in any way and he cowered, literally, before neighbors and friends whom he had known before.[1]

Abandonment is so primal that if it occurs early in development it will impact on all aspects of an individual's life. In seeking a source for the origin of pathological behavior, asking about having experienced abandonment is often fruitful.

For parents of newborns, the baby's cry means it is either hungry, wet, or needs to be comforted. This simple cry, the baby quickly learns, results in relief and, until about six weeks of age, is used as the sole method of motivating parental action. Then something miraculous happens, the baby smiles. It is a smile of recognition and means "I am not abandoned and my discomfort will be removed." It causes the mother to feel attached in a different way. This smile is a new motivation for the mother. The baby is conditioning his or her mother to seek these rewards. A cry and a smile are powerful forces that motivate and shape mother-and-child attachment. The infant starts life as the great natural manipulator, and both the baby and the mother are biologically driven participants.

As the child grows older, when his or her needs are not met, a new form of communication is devised. It is anger, and we call it a tantrum. From about 1½ to 3 years of age, his or her neediness is manifest and, without language, can often go unmet. This leads to frustration for both the mother and child. But this soon passes as language develops and, with it, the child's ability to remember and delay gratification. It is during this time we become toilet trained.

Childhood can be a fertile source of traumatization. A child's thinking is both concrete and imaginative. Imagine a parent who frightens you with the threat of a bogeyman—that evil character of supernatural powers who carries naughty children off to who knows where. Imagine you are told you are good for nothing, and then told to pack your bag so you can be sent to the naughty children's home. Imagine the awfulness of a parent, your protector, becoming a predator. Imagine a priest, a teacher, or other figure in whom you have implicit trust becoming someone who hurts you. Where could you hide? Whom could you tell? Where would you be safe? How does one seek safety when there is no safe place? Preceding a divorce where parents argue in front of their children and one then abruptly leaves produces fear and can be traumatizing. Those are the more obvious sources of abandonment trauma, but the simple act of parents going out for an evening at the wrong time may be sufficient.

The achievement of a secure attachment is a much more complex process than avoiding abandonment. This is the process of emotional bonding. Now there is give and take. The child begins to recognize that his or her mother can leave without experiencing a sense of abandonment. Separation anxiety diminishes. The child's and the mother's temperament need to work together for a smooth transition to adulthood. If this does not occur, the potential for the young adult to be unable to modulate emotional responses is present, lowering the threshold to traumatization.

In the extreme, this lack of attachment and nurturing can have devastating effects. Romanian orphanages under Ceausescu allowed parental visits once every six months. Children slept four to a cot, sharing blankets that were soiled, wet with urine, and lice infected. They did not wash because there was no soap or hot water. Children played with dirty needles and violence was rampant. The children were so neglected they showed no emotion at all. The care workers were poorly trained and cruel, giving the orphans less than 10 minutes of attention a day.[2] The torn cribs had bars and resembled solitary confinement. Their development was physically and emotionally delayed. The age at adoption correlated with the severity of developmental delay. The oldest were seriously impaired. After adoption, 36% had problems of socialization requiring professional intervention.

My father was an angry man. Things, small things, could set off his rage and I would be beaten. As a very young child, I remember him chopping wood with an axe and he had a look on his face (I thought he was thinking about something that made him mad) that frightened me. I was afraid to express my anger toward him.

In 1979, at the age of 10, I went to have an operation on my left foot. A bone needed to be fused to prevent the development of arthritis. Two weeks before surgery, I fell out of a tree house, breaking my nose and knocking myself out. My brother, who thought I was dead, ran across the field to get my father. I came to and was evidently screaming and I remember my father telling me that he stopped running once he heard my screaming.

I was taken to the hospital and just dropped off by my father. I had two black eyes and a broken nose.

The day of the foot surgery I was given a pill that made me very drowsy and I awoke alone in a very dark recovery room full of pain. I'm not sure how long I spent there. I do know that they would not medicate me for the pain because of my age. This enraged me but I was helpless. After that week I was dropped off at boarding school with my foot in plaster.

Since that time, till today, 30 years later, I cannot touch the scar on my foot or even look at it. If someone talks about it, it begins to hurt and I feel nauseous. If I have bare feet, I have to roll up my pant leg so that the bottom of the pant leg won't rub on my scar. I have spent agonizing sessions in therapy trying to talk about the scar and why I feel this way. Trouble is, to talk about it is excruciatingly painful. I do not eat before a therapy session because I feel sick when talking about it. Even to write about it is painful.

Parents who lack nurturing skills due to mental illness or substance abuse cause great havoc in households. Children cannot understand their parent's unpredictable behavior. These children are frightened, confused, and always under stress. Abuse and abandonment by a parent in childhood is always devastating. The lack of a nurturing figure is of immense consequence. To paraphrase Walt Whitman, childhood is the father to the man. Nothing could be truer.

Later-in-Life Causes

Motor vehicle accidents, falling down stairs, being called fat, or being learning disabled can be traumatizing. All forms of betrayal, failure or loss, can be traumatizing. Combat can be traumatizing.

My brother returned from the war Iraq. He was a different person. He would always be in a daze. At home he could not sit comfortably next to a window. If he was near a window, he was very alert, looking out as if something was about to happen. He said the enemy could come through a window. There were times when I found him sleeping on the floor because the bed was near a window and any noise would scare him. A friend of his from the Army had the same reaction. I offered him a seat and he said, "I'd rather stand because I am prepared."

There were days when my brother would be so paranoid that if he heard a noise, he would start screaming things like "Go for cover, they're shooting, enemy alert!" Other times he would just go on talking about the people he killed, including children, and he would break down and cry.

Now when we went to the stores or just for a walk he would be looking up at the buildings and the roofs and say, "You never know who's watching your every move to kill you." There was a time when we heard a firecracker and he freaked out, yelling at everyone in the house to close the windows and stay away from him. We had to remind him he was safe, but safe, he felt, he could never be.

Being given a potentially fatal diagnosis stops all other information from being processed and is often traumatizing. A doctor's words or his or her indifference can cut deeper and have longer lasting scars than any knife. The legal system is no different; victims of crimes such as rape and assault are often blamed for being provocative. Just when support is needed most, the victim feels abandoned and sometimes made to feel guilty and ashamed.

Cultural Sources

Trauma sources are not just personal. The Great Depression was a source where family men were traumatized by loss of their jobs and their role as providers. Today, many highly successful people who grew up during that time now hoard possessions and are frugal—just in case. During those terrible times President Roosevelt provided a brilliant solution. He put people to work and promised something that was genius. He promised Social Security. This program allowed men not to feel terrified that their families would go hungry and allowed families to remain together.

When a haven does not exist, there is the potential for traumatization. The great plague of the Middle Ages was a source for traumatization, as was 9/11, made infinitely worse by repeated showing of the event and by the misguided color threat system where red meant high alert and green meant safety. Where could one find a haven?

Since September 11, 2001, I suffered extreme anxiety and have had difficulty sleeping. Each night I would lie awake, watching airplanes fly up the

Hudson River through my bedroom window. Each time one took a flight path I thought to be too low, I would jump out of bed, scurry to my living room, and watch the plane, waiting to see if I needed to wake my family for a quick exit. I thought for sure one of these planes would eventually come straight for my building. I visualized it happening and lived that dreadful moment over and over in my mind.

Slavery was a great source of traumatization, the Holocaust was a great source of traumatization, the destruction of the Native Americans was a great source of traumatization, and through the ages, there were many other societal moments where fear and anger were real and havens did not exist. Thus, not only are there moments that affect the individual, but entire cultures, races, and nationalities can be affected by events.

The media is a constant source of traumatization. Through television and other media outlets, we witness horrific things as they are happening. Its reach is so large that it is arguably the most important source of fear. There are reasons children should not watch certain things until they can place them into perspective.

Being traumatized can inhibit one from seeking a haven. Children who are physically, emotionally, and sexually abused often have difficulty seeking a haven because of shame, anger, and guilt. Battered women, the isolated elderly, and the homeless all may suffer from traumatization and be unable to find a safe place.

With so many potential causes, how is it we do not all experience the consequences of traumatization? The truth is, to a greater or lesser extent, we do.

Consequences of Traumatization

Why?

> Why had Pamela's right hand been killing her for the last three months? She hadn't hurt it, nor was there any sign she accidentally injured it. It was very tender to the touch.
>
> Why couldn't John sleep? Since 9/11, whenever he heard a plane, he would jump out of bed to see if the flight would end up in his apartment.
>
> Why couldn't Mary get on an airplane?

Why wouldn't Joseph speak in public?

Why did Jane have episodes where she couldn't breathe and felt she was going to die?

Why was Arthur too frightened to drive?

Why would Sarah walk up 20 flights rather than use the elevator?

Why couldn't Arnold walk?

Why couldn't Peter sleep near a window and preferred sleeping on the floor of the kitchen after returning from a tour of duty in Iraq?

Why did Joseph have chronic back pain that does not respond to treatment?

Why was Samantha unable to stop mourning her mother's death?

Why did Frank stutter?

While all aspects of life can be affected by traumatization, there are six named disorders where the primary pathology can be traced to being encoded in the amygdala. We call these disorders of traumatization or amygdala-based disorders.

Amygdala-Based Disorders

Phobias
Panic
PTSD
Pathological emotions
Pain
Somatization

Phobias

Phobias provide a model for the simplest form of amygdala-based traumatization. A phobia produces a fear response to objects and situations that are not inherently threatening. There is no evolutionary advantage to be terrified of public speaking or escalators or the number 13. Certainly airplanes, cars, tunnels, and bridges did not exist during early human evolution, so why do some people become terrified at the mere thought of these objects or circumstances? Since there is no innate danger associated with these objects or situations, phobias should be considered learned (see Appendix C for details of phobia generation).

The generation of a phobia permanently links fear to a stimulus. Perception of this stimulus releases stress neurochemicals and hence meets our definition of traumatization. Phobias are related to the responses that are generated from an unconditioned fear stimulus (UFS). These UFS are nonspecific, falling into broad categories that can be applied to many situations. As described earlier, such stimuli are reflective of the many ways we can be killed or hurt and are hard-wired in the brain. They include fear of the unknown (novel situations), heights (falling), closed spaces (being trapped), being unable to run, open places (no place to hide), creepy-crawly slithery things (land-based predators), and something coming from outside of our visual field (air-based predator). As mammals we also can develop a fear of being abandoned, of being alone, known as autophobia.

Phobia Generation and Generalization

Phobia generation requires the four elements to be present. You are riding along in a car and go over a bridge; you look down and see how high you are off the ground. In the susceptible individual, the height, a UFS, produces an innate fear response. In addition, you are unable to escape because you are riding in a car on the bridge. However, since you are consciously aware you are crossing a bridge, the bridge then becomes associated with the fear response generated by the UFS. In a bridge phobia, the rational prefrontal cortex is unable to shut off the fear because it is not the bridge (the conditioned stimulus) that is activating the fear response; it is the fear of heights (the UFS).

When crossing another bridge, because of a similarity of overlap of the surroundings, your fear of bridges generalizes.

Pattern Recognition and Generalizability

Why does a traumatized fear generalize? Why does someone who is afraid of crossing a bridge become afraid of all bridges? Then become afraid of tunnels, crowds, flying, and eventually develop agoraphobia, the fear of being outside? There are two reasons. The first is that traumatization begets traumatization. A traumatized landscape is primed for further traumatization, but not all go on to this end. The other reason, which is the topic of this essay, is that by nature's design, the mind seeks similarities in situations. This allows for rapid assessment of a potentially threatening situation. While our mind searches a novel situation for similarities, our vigilance system is activated and prepares us. If there are similarities, previously encoded responses are activated. A phobia of bridges activates the fear system for any bridge. This widening of the traumatization occurs by pattern recognition processing. Even a small piece of this novel situation overlapping with the original encoding event may be enough to activate the amygdala.

A plant is perceived because it has a stem, a flower, leaves, color, smell, and comes up from the ground. The perception is the sum of these various component parts, sent via the thalamus to the various brain areas dealing with specific sensory information, and then, somehow, binds to become a plant in our consciousness. Seeing only pieces of a flower, a petal, a leaf, a stem, can produce in the mind the entire flower. This can be conceptualized as the brain performing a rapid matching function, looking for similar pieces already stored in the brain. We often say that this looks or smells or tastes like something familiar. (Lots of stuff tastes like chicken!) Indeed, we illustrate much of life with simile. Our brain seeks these congruent patterns in unfamiliar circumstances. Part of why we experience déjà vu is because of pattern overlap that provides a sense of familiarity.

Pattern recognition is the way in which the brain matches sensory input to create a perception. A percept is a high-level representation of part of the world as imaged by the brain based on a set of rules. This percept is then amplified or diminished by our current state of attention and previous experience. Pattern recognition processing, from sensory input to perception to response, occurs for both conscious and subconscious patterns. If the pattern has enough overlap with an encoded event, it may elicit a fear response from the amygdala. This constitutes a potential mechanism for the generalization of a fear response.

Paul had a phobia of statues. This bizarre phobia arose when, as a child, he saw a bust of the head of the crucified Christ, complete with a crown of thorns and showing His immense suffering. This traumatized him. This is an example of vicarious traumatization. He then generalized this fear to all statues.

Panic Attacks

A panic attack is characterized by sudden attacks of terror, usually accompanied by a pounding heart, weakness, faintness, or dizziness. During these attacks, people may feel flushed or chilled; their hands may tingle or they may feel numb. They may become short of breath, experience chest pain, and feel they are going to die. They often experience a sense of unreality, a fear of impending doom and imminent death, or a fear of losing control of their mind. Individuals who experience panic attacks can't predict where or when an attack will occur and will always avoid a situation where an attack has happened. Many worry intensely about the next attack. Panic attacks can occur at any time, even during sleep. They are a frequent cause for emergency room visits.

Panic attacks most often begin in late adolescence and are more common in women than men. Not everyone who has a panic attack goes on to have multiple attacks that lead to a diagnosis of panic disorder. A strong tendency to inherit this disorder is known. Some people with panic disorder become so restricted by their fears that they avoid normal activities, such as grocery shopping or driving. About one-third become housebound or are able to confront a feared situation only when accompanied by a spouse or other trusted person. Both phobias and panic disorder produce irrational fears.

The remarkable aspect of panic disorder is the lack of any warning and the absence of any cognitive cue. This is unusual because a fear response is usually generated in preparation for escape from something we are aware of. This does not happen here. Thus, the stimulus that initiates the panic attack is subconscious. It is likely that fear of an unanticipated attack plays a major role in sensitizing the individual and making the situation worse. In this disorder, there truly is no haven.

What role does the amygdala play in panic disorder?[3] Research shows that most of the neurons in to the basolateral complex (BLC) of the amygdala inhibits the flow toward the central nucleus (Ce). It is speculated that in panic disorder, this inhibition is somehow diminished and activation of Ce occurs at a much lower threshold. Thus, mild, anxiety-provoking internal stimuli, such as a rapid heartbeat, chest pain, or lightheadedness, which would not normally engage the amygdala, do so, causing the Ce to activate other areas of the brain, producing a fear response. Since no "predator" is seen, the situation is inescapable. People experience great dread because they cannot locate the source of fear. This repeating cycle of subconscious stimuli and severe fear landscapes the amygdala and produces a more generalized fear of the outside world. It is notable that being at home seems to prevent these attacks, except perhaps when sleeping, during which the mind can experience anything.

Posttraumatic Stress Disorder (PTSD)

PTSD is considered to be the prototype of traumatization. Individuals with PTSD present with a complex array of symptoms that include:

Reexperiencing the trauma
Emotional numbing
Avoidance
Increased arousal (hypervigilance)
Diminished capacity for problem solving
Nightmares, flashbacks, and intrusive thoughts
Repetition compulsion

Since some of these symptoms seem opposite from the others, this disorder seems puzzling. How can one be emotionally numb at one moment, then experience increased arousal at the next? PTSD may be diagnosed months after an event has been traumatized, as the internal response to subconscious and conscious cues or other events causing chronic stress altering the landscape of the brain allows for the production of symptoms. According to our model, for a traumatization to occur, only the conditions outlined earlier need to be met; however, some researchers feel that PTSD has a unique aspect: The individual often is unable to give a complete narrative of the event causing the disorder. PTSD contains a cognitively mental imprint of sensory and affective elements of the traumatic experience.

Most researchers believe the components of the traumatic memory are stored in different memory systems. That is, the cognitive, emotional, and somatosensory components are not anatomically located together. The complete picture must be assembled from different parts of the brain. It is felt the amygdala is the structure that establishes associations between these components. In fact, traumatization can be looked upon as a disorder of permanent association and, in extreme cases like PTSD, a disorder of partial association or, in other words, dissociation. It is by disrupting the normal amygdala/hippocampal function to protect us from encoding consciously available memories that are too horrible that we develop PTSD. It has been suggested earlier that very high levels of cortisol at the time of the event are the cause of a disrupted narrative, making some memories unavailable to conscious recall. It may be that disordered retrieval is at the heart of PTSD. PTSD is often progressive, as more of the narrative is revealed from the subconscious in flashbacks, intrusive thoughts, and dreams. Unless this process can be disrupted, the extreme fear arising from this activation of the amygdala often makes things worse. One important and interesting consequence of PTSD is a disorder called repetition compulsion.

Repetition Compulsion

The range of problems traumatization can produce is remarkable. One of the most extraordinary is the compulsive self-exposure of the traumatized individual to the experience of trauma again. Research shows that physically abused children are more likely to reexperience a similar trauma later in life. Some become abusers themselves. Many prostitutes have been sexually molested as children. Repetition compulsion[4] is about the individual subconsciously reenacting the trauma. This underscores the power of the homeostatically driven need to heal. Sadly, because the person is unsure why he or she is being driven to exhibit this behavior, a safe haven can never be found. This repetition does not help a person gain mastery of the situation; rather, it often reinforces the insolvability of the problem, making the need to reenact even more powerful.

PTSD, as well as the other amygdala-based disorders, appears to require a certain landscape for symptoms to occur. Thus, symptoms may be delayed by days, months, or even years after a traumatizing event. This landscape can be created by the addition of chronic stress.

In the case of PTSD, this landscape can be the result of the event itself or other unrelated life stressors.

Chronic Pain

Most Western medicine is end-organ driven. That is, if you have a back problem, the problem is considered to be in the back; a pelvic problem must originate in the pelvis. Indeed, Western medicine names these problems by the end organ; thus, we have "lower back pain" and "pelvic floor dysfunction." This approach is called **physicalism**. Therefore, if a patient experiences a physical problem, the problem must have a physical origin. Of course, surgery and other traditional Western approaches can definitely treat many physical problems, but practitioners also find problems for which no, or only partial, solutions are available from a physical standpoint.

That chronic pain can be psychological in origin is hard for most people to comprehend. It makes sense that when we touch a spot that feels tender, the cause of the pain must arise somewhere near that spot. This is not always true. The somatic parts (pain, burning, temperature alterations, and tenderness) of a trauma can be stored in the brain to be retrieved by exposure to subconscious stimuli, processed through the BLC, and reperceived.

$$\text{Subconscious stimuli} \rightarrow \text{BLC} \rightarrow \text{Ce} \rightarrow \text{Pain}$$

The Ce of the amygdala has a pain center called the nociceptive amygdala. It is here that pain signals arriving from other parts of the brain are modulated. During flight, fight, or rage, inhibition by norepinephrine of the nociceptive (pain-perceiving) portion of the Ce prevents the pain from being experienced.

If one consciously evokes a painful traumatic event and generates the emotional component, the somatic pain experience is not elicited due to the release of norepinephrine (NE) and its effect on the Ce. Thus, thinking about the event does not cause pain. This is what makes this pain syndrome so confusing.

$$\text{Consciously evoked emotional event-related stimuli} \rightarrow \text{BLC} \rightarrow$$
$$\text{Ce} \rightarrow \uparrow \text{NE} \rightarrow \text{No pain}$$

Regardless of the exact network of neurons involved, the pain occurring during the traumatizing event is stored as a memory in the brain. This was first described in the late 1800s by Charcot, Janet, Freud, and Breuer who believed subconscious stimuli could cause pain and other somatic symptoms. They believed the pain was coencoded with a psychological trauma but cognitively dissociated from conscious awareness. Accordingly, pain relief would occur only when the trauma was brought to conscious awareness and treated.

In addition to traumatically encoded fearful events as a cause of pain and other somatic sensations, John Sarno[5] suggests that symptoms arise to prevent traumatically encoded subconscious rage and other negative emotions from reaching consciousness. The inability to express strong negative emotions can come from fear of punishment, helplessness, the need to be in control, and the need to be seen as the 'good one.' It is interesting to note that the areas where pain is most commonly described are the back, neck, head, and upper limbs. Many of these individuals also grind their teeth and clench their jaws. Remarkably, these are also the locations of the muscles described for use during defensive rage. This triad of neck pain, back pain, and temporomandibular joint syndrome is very common in clinical practice.

On the Origin of Chronic Psychogenic Pain

This essay attempts to produce a model for understanding chronic pain as it occurs in traumatization. Quite often, during a traumatizing event where bodily injury occurs, we do not experience pain. The question then arises: If pain was not experienced at the time of the event, how does chronic pain based on the event develop later? The case in which a woman's hand was hurting for three months is illustrative. The patient was injured in a taxi accident in London, where the vehicle overturned. As the car tumbled, her hand swung wildly in the car. The back of her hand was badly bruised, but she did not experience the pain at the time of the accident. The pain and tenderness returned 15 years later, when she had decided to return to London to live.

The physiology at work here can be explained as follows. During the event, norepinephrine was secreted into the amygdala from the locus

coeruleus. Flight was not possible during the event, and the four crite-
ria, including inescapability, were present, which led to a traumatiza-
tion. Norepinephrine (NE) release at the time of the event inhibited the
nociceptive Ce from signaling pain to consciousness (Pain from hand
goes to brain → ↑ NE → Ce → // Consciousness). From a survival point
of view this makes sense, as her first priority was to escape from the
overturned vehicle. Each and every time she would consciously recall
the event, norepinephrine would be released, inhibiting the conscious
awareness of pain.

Her desire to return to London had enough overlap with the
context of the event to stimulate the BLC regarding the event.
Norepinephrine was not generated because the thought of retuning to
London was not in and of itself threatening. Not only did she experi-
ence pain, but she also felt tenderness of the area, suggesting that local
effects were being produced. Since she was not consciously thinking of
the event, her clues that would associate the event with the pain were
absent.

It appears that coencoded subconscious contextual stimuli can selec-
tively activate the pain pathway without activating either the emo-
tional or cognitive components of the traumatizing event. Havening
the emotional component of distress on recall of the taxi accident broke
the linkages that BLC → Event and BLC → Pain had in common. As
the coencoded subconscious stimulus used this pathway to produce pain,
her pain disappeared after havening.

If one consciously thinks about the pain and applies havening, it may
be possible to inhibit the BLC pathway responsible for that specific pain.
If, however, the cognitive-emotional linkage is not broken, the poten-
tial exists to reexperience pain encoded, often elsewhere in the body. This
model is also true for chronic pain involving rage. Unrelated events that
produce anger or stress may overlap with the encoded rage and reproduce
the neck, jaw, and lower back muscle tension.

Somatosensory conditions that can be coencoded with trauma
include:

Low back pain
Neck and upper back pain
Sciatica

Somatization disorders
Radiculopathies
Phantom limb pain
Temporomandibular joint syndrome
Chest pain

Nonetheless, for both patients and health care professionals, this chronic pain is perceived as arising from peripheral sites. Thus, much therapeutic effort is directed to these areas, including treatments with opioid analgesia, surgery, and physical therapy. Unfortunately, these meet with little success.

Pathological Emotions

The pathological emotions, including guilt, shame, jealousy, grief, and so on, are reflective emotional states. They require a strong degree of attachment. Guilt, as in Lady Macbeth's cry to remove the blood from her hands, can be experienced in dreams or in the awake state.

At first Sandra did not understand their young daughter's diagnosis of autism, given to her by her pediatrician. When she heard it the second time from an expert, she was landscaped for traumatization. She felt guilty she may have done something wrong during pregnancy (she did not), she experienced anger about this happening to her child, and she experienced fear that her child would need lifelong care. She experienced grief over the loss of the expectations of this new relationship. These emotions were her daily fare. She used food as a way to treat her emotions. She gained over 100 pounds during the next several years. Nonetheless, she functioned as a loving, caring mother, but with a heavy heart (and body).

The traumatization of pathological emotions may seem like a normal response to a tragedy, but these emotions produce chronic stress and alter the nature of all relationships. They may prevent the mourning process from occurring. This maladaptive behavior continues as long as the cue and content, in this case her guilt, fear, and subconscious anger, stimulate the amygdala and release stress hormones. These pathological emotions produce a landscape of the brain that sets the stage for further traumatization.

Somatization

There is another form of an amygdala-based disorder described in the psychiatric literature. It produces an astonishing array of symptoms. These symptoms are called somatization responses and represent a somatosensory/autonomic response to the event. For example, survivors who witnessed the killings by the Khmer Rouge lost their ability to see.[6] All were women who witnessed violent acts, such as seeing their daughters being raped and beaten to death by soldiers, or their husbands or sons being executed in front of them.

Some somatic symptoms can be very puzzling, such as stigmata. Here, the markings of Christ on the cross appear on the body of the individual. It is not a leap of faith to see how someone can be traumatized by seeing an image of the Crucifixion. Clearly, these individuals are highly susceptible. Stigmata may appear on the body as the somatic response to subconscious retrieval of a traumatizing memory (imagine the fear that must be generated in children when seeing a crucified man on a cross and who are too young to understand it) and be expressed via the autonomic nervous system as vasomotor dysregulation in the areas of Christ's injuries.

Somatization of a traumatic event can produce blindness, paralysis, stuttering, copious vaginal secretions, pelvic floor dysfunction, vomiting, stuffy nose, and literally an almost endless array of distressing problems. These symptoms should always initiate a search for a traumatic event. It is here that a cure may be found.

After being sexually assaulted, Stephanie developed copious vaginal secretions, up to 50 cc/day, that prevented her from leaving the house. She ultimately required surgery to remove the vaginal wall.

Other Consequences of Traumatization

The consequences of traumatization are extraordinarily varied. As mentioned above, phobias, somatization disorders, panic, chronic pain, chronic emotional states, and PTSD are consequences of traumatization. It is highly likely traumatization impacts other disorders by altering the landscape. Diseases such as depression, anxiety, substance abuse, obsessive-compulsive disorder, and so on, may have some component that relates to traumatization.[7] These consequences arise from a maladaptive response to chronic stress. This maladaptive response affects various brain systems, such as the nucleus accumbens (associated with addictive disorders), cingulate gyrus (associated with disorders of emotional regulation), and caudate nucleus (associated with compulsive disorders).[8] Traumatization may even be passed to your descendents.[9]

The Absence of Forgetting

The persistence of a traumatic memory is puzzling. While it is true that nontraumatized emotional moments can often be recalled, they are not usually so vivid and associated with intense emotions. Nor are there somatic and autonomic components. As observed by Janet, traumatized memories are accurate and immutable over time; he believed they are fixed in the subconscious. Nontraumatized memories, on the other hand, can change. When a haven cannot be found or an escape cannot be perceived at the moment of traumatization, we never feel safe; the threat, concomitant vigilance, and feelings are always with us.

One possible explanation is that during initial amygdala activation by a perceived threat, the prefrontal cortex (PFC) is inhibited from sending an inhibitory signal to the amygdala. This inhibitory signal is known to release GABA in the amygdala. When an event is synaptically encoded as a traumatization, there is no perceived escape and no signal is sent to the amygdala from the prefrontal cortex. This lack of signal allows for the potentiation of the glutamate pathway, the moment is encoded and the memory endures, readily available for reactivation. Subsequent recall of a component of a previously traumatized event by thought or other stimuli causes the BLC to send an inhibitory signal to the prefrontal cortex, ensuring that the pathway is not erased.

Treating the traumatized memory requires discovering the origin of the emotional core of a traumatization. Since the emotional distress from recall of a traumatically encoded moment is experienced as if it were occurring for the first time, this suggests that if a neurobiological equivalent of safety can be generated after emotional activation, the pathway can be disrupted.

References

1. Robertson, J. (1962). *Hospitals and children: A parent's-eye view* (pp. 57–58). New York, NY: Gollancz.
2. Ames, E. W. (1997). *The development of Romanian orphanages children adopted to Canada*. Ottawa, Canada: Human Resources Development. Retrieved from http://findarticles.com/p/articles/mi_m2248/is_136_34/ai_59810232/
3. Shekhar, A., Sajdyk, T. S., Keim, S. R., Yoder, K. K., & Sanders, S. K. (1999). Role of basolateral amygdala in panic disorder. *Ann. N.Y. Acad. Sci.* 747–750.
4. van der Kolk, B. A. (1989). The compulsion to repeat trauma. *Psychiatr. Clin. North Am.* 12(2):389–411.
5. Sarno, J. E. (2006). *The divided mind*, pp. 89–128. New York, NY: Regan Books.
6. Smith, A. (1989, September 8). *Long Beach Journal:* Eyes that saw horrors now see only shadows. Special to the *New York Times*.
7. Felitti, V. J., Anda, R. F., Nordenberg, D., Williamson, D. F., Spitz, A. M., Edwards, V., Koss, M. P., & Marks, J. B. Relationship of childhood abuse and household dysfunction to many of the leading causes of death in adults: The Adverse Childhood Experiences (ACE) Study (1998). *Am. J. Prev. Med.* 14(4): 245–258. For an up to date analysis see http://www.cdc.gov/nccdphp/ace/
8. Scaer, R. C. (2005). *The trauma spectrum: Hidden wounds and human resiliency*. New York, NY: W.W. Norton Press.
9. www.developingchild.net working paper#10.

7

DISRUPTING A TRAUMATIZATION

Traumatization can be avoided if, during a potentially traumatizing moment, an escape is perceived. If an event is encoded as a traumatic memory, upon recall of the event, providing the individual with a safe haven should disrupt the trauma-induced linkages and erase the emotional response to related stimuli.

Avoiding the Encoding of a Traumatic Memory

A gang of thugs is chasing you after you inadvertently insulted the leader's girlfriend. They are going to beat you to a pulp after they catch you and you are literally running for your life. You are getting tired and there is no place to hide. The thugs are gaining and your heart is racing as fast as it can to keep you going. They are just about to catch you and all of a sudden you wake up. Sweating, eyes wide open, and heart pumping, you realize it was just a dream and you laugh to yourself, but it's a little hard getting back to sleep. Awakening just in time from a scary dream is a great way to escape the danger and avoid traumatization. Escape is when the danger has permanently passed. Hollywood understands this concept. How many endings of scary movies have you seen where the predator, thought to be killed, somehow manages to survive and look the audience in the face? Just when you thought you were safe, that you escaped—it is the stuff nightmares and traumatizations are made of.

At the beginning of a potentially traumatizing event, when specific pathways are being created, it is unclear whether the criteria for inescapability will be met. At this moment, dopamine, norepinephrine, and cortisol are elevated, preparing us to do what needs to be done to survive. If we survive and find a haven we calm down. To calm down, we need to inhibit the release of norepinephrine from the locus coeruleus (LC) and inhibit the central nucleus (Ce) from further activating our physiology. In the LC, serotonin via its effect on GABA neurons prevents the release of norepinephrine.[1] The prefrontal cortex, on perceiving the threat has passed, inhibits the Ce via GABA interneurons. The amygdala is now quiet and the event fades. But things are different if an event is encoded as a trauma.

Disrupting an Encoded Trauma

Once an event has been encoded as a traumatization, the subsequent finding of a haven does not disrupt the pathways. How, then, do we de-encode a traumatic memory? The answer is to disrupt the synaptically encoded glutamate-specific pathways in the basolateral complex (BLC). To do so, we must seek the event that leads to their activation, for as we have mentioned earlier, once activated, the glutamate receptors become vulnerable to disruption. Then, once activated, fool the brain into thinking a haven has been found. To promote this, we must also inhibit the cognitive component from further activating the amygdala. The path to a cure is outlined below:

Retrieval of emotional component → Working memory → Hippocampus → Activate BLC → ↓ Sensory input of the event to the amygdala by distraction → Havening → Disrupt the encoded emotional BLC pathway by depotentiation of glutamate receptors → De-link the components of the traumatization → Traumatization cured

Preventing the Passage of a Retrieved Component From Working Memory to the Amygdala

Conscious/subconscious retrieval of a traumatized component en route to the amygdala passes through a system known as **working memory** (WM) (Figure 7.1). The working memory system (generally considered to be part of the prefrontal cortex) receives the stored memories and sends this information to the hippocampus. If this information has been encoded as part of a traumatization, it is forwarded to the

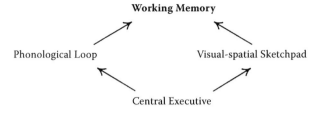

Figure 7.1   Working memory. (Courtesy of Ronald Ruden and Steve Lampasona.)

amygdala. The WM system is a limited-capacity store for retrieving and retaining information over the short term that allows for performing mental operations on the contents of the store. According to Baddeley,[2] working memory has, at minimum, two components, a **phonological loop** that is concerned with auditory and speech-based information, and the **visual-spatial sketchpad** that maintains and manipulates visual and spatial information. His model also postulates a **central executive** that directs what working memory pays attention to and supervises these two components. The central executive's role is to regulate attention, and it does not readily allow working memory to hold dissimilar items simultaneously.

Displacing From Working Memory a Stimulus That Activates the BLC

Working memory is the system to which retrieved components of the traumatic memory are first brought. In order to keep the component in working memory, it must be rehearsed or augmented by an emotional feeling. The ability of an emotion-producing stimulus to sustain the item in working memory is the reason feelings can overwhelm rational thought. However, even emotion-producing stimuli that enter the working memory system can be displaced if the mind is distracted. Displacement can be accomplished by simultaneously attending to other cognitive or physical tasks. Using Baddeley's model, after entry into the working memory, having the individual attend to verbal commands that activate the visual-spatial sketchpad (having them imagine walking downstairs while counting the steps) or the auditory loop (hum "Take Me Out to the Ball Game") can displace the component. It is nearly impossible for the mind to sustain two different items in working memory. Try for yourself by adding two 3-digit numbers in your head while humming the "Star Spangled Banner." For the moment, this displacement stops the retrieved traumatic memory from activating the amygdala and producing a response. However, it requires a concentrated effort to do so.

Working memory can only hold one item.

Traumatic component in WM → Displacement from WM → → /////// Hippocampus → ////// BLC activation → No response

The displacement of the traumatic component from working memory temporarily extinguishes the response.

If the working memory is holding an event that activates the emotional component, it is difficult to dislodge it, and even if dislodged, it returns at another time. Nonetheless, if one can displace the event, activation of the BLC will cease. Thus, for example, for someone who is snake phobic, bringing into working memory an image of a slithering, sliding snake will cause the release of norepinephrine and a fear response. Distraction by thinking of something else stops this conscious activation of the BLC. However, bringing another snake to WM will reactivate the BLC and cause the person to reexperience the fear response.

Shakespeare expressed the idea that retrieval of traumatic memories causes us to reexperience the feelings as if for the first time, and that we can alter these feelings by displacement from working memory:

Sonnet 30

> When to the sessions of sweet silent thought
> I summon up remembrance of things past,
> I sigh the lack of many a thing I sought,
> And with old woes new wail my dear time's waste:
> Then can I drown an eye, unused to flow,
> For precious friends hid in death's dateless night,
> And weep afresh love's long since cancelled woe,
> And moan the expense of many a vanished sight.
> Then can I grieve at grievances foregone,

And heavily from woe to woe tell o'er
The sad account of fore-bemoanèd moan,
Which I new pay as if not paid before.
But if the while I think on thee, dear friend,
All losses are restored and sorrows end.

Activating Traumatic Components So They Can Be Treated

In order to disrupt a traumatic memory, it must first be retrieved and brought into working memory. Then it must activate the BLC. This activation corresponds to the release of glutamate in the BLC-specific pathway that was produced during encoding. It is this ability of stimuli to activate the BLC pathway that must be de-encoded. This prevents a signal from being sent to the Ce (which in turn activates the locus coeruleus and releases norepinephrine) and the other areas of the brain where the linkages are stored. In the case of subconscious stimuli that activate somatosensory and autonomic symptoms, bringing the symptom into working memory followed by havening may rid the individual of the symptoms, but it will not eliminate the synaptic pathway through the BLC that encodes the emotional response. The ability to reencode these nonemotional components exists and relapse remains possible. Sarno[3] has observed this in many of his patients, symptoms returning or appearing elsewhere if the emotional core was not disrupted.

To de-traumatize an event we must search for its emotional origin so that it can be activated. A diagnosis of an amygdala-based disorder should make us seek the encoding event. Chronic pain and other somatic symptoms should cause us to search for a traumatizing event or unresolved anger. PTSD has both cognitive and subconscious stimuli that activate the emotions, and all should be sought. Phobias directly enter into working memory by cognitive processes and activate a fear response. Trying to recall the first time it happened is helpful. Pathological emotions arising from distressing events can be directly activated by conscious effort. If no origin can be found, such as in panic attacks, one can still generate emotions for panic disorder by thinking about the last time it occurred and how fearful we are that it will happen again. Even events that are not cognitively stored, such as those from early childhood, can be de-traumatized if we can recreate the felt sense, the emotion and/or some sensory feeling. If the traumatizing event can be found and activated, this affords an opportunity to alter the BLC pathway. How can this be accomplished?

Early Successful Trauma Treatments

Early attempts at treating the consequences of a traumatization by talk therapy were generally unsuccessful. Most researchers felt that a traumatization permanently encoded the event, and that cognitive cues or subconscious triggers of the event caused emotional, somatosensory, and visceral responses derived from the original trauma. Professionals in this field thought that a cure was not possible. As we shall see, this has proved to be wrong.

Dr. Roger Callahan first described his tapping approach to cure trauma in 1985.[4] This was followed by eye movement desensitization and reprocessing (EMDR), described by Dr. Francine Shapiro.[5] Both therapies involve imaginal reexposure to the event and followed by various forms of sensory input. Dr. Callahan's approach was to evoke the memory of the trauma, then tap on various acupuncture points. This would be interspersed with a distracting process called a Gamut procedure. EMDR has eight phases. These phases include reexposure and maintenance of the images while attending to other forms of stimulation in the form of repeated sets of eye movements, tones, and taps. The goal is to focus on the information, as it is currently stored. In well-controlled trials, EMDR was shown to cure PTSD in a significant percentage of patients.

Somatic experiencing is a method for the treatment of trauma described by Dr. Peter Levine.[5] He focused his therapeutic efforts on the moments when a traumatizing event is encoded and uses an escape metaphor to describe his theory. It is of interest here because he recognizes that finding an escape is critical for the resolution of a traumatized event. According to Levine,[6] "Traumatic symptoms are not caused by the triggering event itself. They stem from the frozen residue of energy that has not been resolved and discharged; this residue remains trapped in the nervous system where it can wreck havoc on our bodies and spirit. It occurs because we cannot complete the process of moving in, through and out of the 'immobility' or freezing state." (Dr. Levine and Dr. Scaer (see below) use the term *freeze state* to denote flaccidity.) He uses the animal model of "freeze discharge" to free the individual from the traumatic event. After attempting escape and being caught, an animal becomes flaccid. If somehow the animal survives, it begins to move its legs as if it were running. This is the freeze discharge. After a few moments, the animal is then able to get up and walk away.

Traumatization occurred when the animal could not experience a freeze discharge. For Levine, the animal is psychologically and physically frozen in time. How does one escape from this state? Levine says this is possible by accessing the "felt sense," that which is stored in the procedural memory system. This can be done by a variety of ways, not always requiring the recall of the event. Just sensing the inescapability may be sufficient. Levine[7] uses Eugene Gendlin's term *felt sense*, which "is not a mental experience but a physical one. Physical. A bodily awareness of a situation or person or event. An internal aura that encompasses everything you feel and know about the given subject at a given time—encompasses it and communicates it to you all at once."

This felt sense is the gut feeling, the knowing without knowledge, the experience of correctness or incorrectness; it is somatosensory information without interpretation. It is the physical aspects of emotion without cognition. The same pathway that is activated by cognitive generation of emotions is also activated and experienced as a felt sense.

The first step in somatic experiencing is to retrieve the feeling aspect of the event. The next step is to complete an escape that liberates the undischarged energy. In his seminal story, Levine encourages the patient to run when fear arises. This completes the escape, a freeze discharge has occurred, albeit in the client's imagination, and the person is cured. His discovery story is wonderfully instructive[8]:

> As I began with this patient she began to relax. Suddenly, without warning, she panicked. Terrified, and with no notion of what to do, I had a fleeting image of a tiger jumping towards us. It appeared dreamlike, and at the time, I had no idea where it had come from.

"There is a tiger coming after you, Nancy," "Run toward that tree; climb it and escape." To my amazement, Nancy's body began to shake and tremble. Her legs started making running movements. After several minutes, she took a few spontaneous breaths. This response, which was scary for both of us, washed over her in waves for almost an hour. At the end she experienced a profound calm, saying she felt "held in warm tingly waves."

Nancy reported to me that during this hour she saw mental pictures of herself at the age of three being held down and given ether anesthesia for a tonsillectomy. The fear of suffocation she experienced as a child—and that she remembered and revisited during her session with me was—terrifying. As a child she felt overwhelmed and helpless. After this one session with me, a whole host of debilitating symptoms improved dramatically, and she felt "like had herself again."

Another mind-body exposure approach is called the sensorimotor approach to psychotherapy. Here the somatosensory component is brought to awareness and then treated. Pat Ogden and colleagues[9] describe this process in their book *Trauma and the Body*. In this therapy, talking is not of importance. Neither are the associations, fantasies, narratives, and defenses the individual has. Rather, it is the unregulated body experiences that are the focus of this therapy. For traumatized individuals, although the narrative of the event may be dissociated, the somatic experience is available. Using this approach, the memory can be safely reevoked and empowering actions are executed. These exposure methods use emotions and body sensations to activate the specific glutamate-encoded pathways, causing them to be subject to disruption.

Are there other ways that we can disrupt this encoding?

Disrupting the Amygdala Component of a Traumatic Event: A Neurobiological Mechanism

Early researchers such as Janet and Freud[10] felt that traumatization caused their victims to become fixed in the past, in some cases becoming obsessed with the trauma. Janet observed behaviors and feelings that included nightmares, intense reactions to benign stimuli, terror without reason, and grief without relief to reminder cues arising from the original event. These are people stuck in their past with no escape, for whom the past is always present. These memories do not decrease over time and they elicit responses decades after the event.

Sonia, the daughter of an employee of Homeland Security, heard frightening stories about terrorists and potential threats to the country as she grew up. After getting married, Sonia's husband would be awakened in the night by her screaming. He would find her curled in a fetal position in a corner of the room screaming, yet she was asleep. These are called night terrors (see Appendix D). He couldn't awaken her, and the episode could last several frightening minutes. She didn't recall those moments. Sonia also found that she didn't like to leave the house. She would only go for a walk with her new and very large bulldog. Her life was becoming more and more constricted. It was clear from her history that she could not find a safe place; chased, she could not escape.

A potential model for the disrupting an encoded glutamate pathway comes from Rasolkhani-Kalhorn, Harper, and Drozd, on the mechanism for the efficacy of EMDR and amygdala de-potentiation (see Appendix F). These researchers believed that EMDR disrupted the activated glutamate receptors by a mechanism called de-potentiation. The principal mechanism for depotentiation is the removal, by internalization, of activated glutamate receptors by the production of a low-frequency signal produced by eye movement. These receptors, now internalized within the neuron, cannot transmit a signal and the pathway is disrupted.

Activated BLC glutamate receptor → Eye movements → Induction of low-frequency signal → Depotentiation and internalization of BLC glutamate receptor → Inability to transmit a signal → Traumatic memory disrupted

Are there other forms of sensory input that can accomplish this?

The Extrasensory Response to Touch

The first experiences we have with fear, especially abandonment, seem to respond to touch. What does this touch do? In addition to temperature, vibration, consistency, shape, texture, pressure, and of course pain, touch provides comfort, sensuality, relaxation, and experiences that have nothing to do with the classic neurobiology of ascending pathways. The consequences of the sensation of touch in mammals must therefore affect pathways that involve cognition and emotion.[11] These are the extrasensory properties of touch.

For example, if I stroke the bottom of my foot, or I have a friend stroke the bottom of my foot, the ticklish response is much more intense when my friend strokes it. If someone you hated stroked your head, the response would be much different than someone you loved doing the same thing. So the context of the touching matters, but in the beginning, right after birth, a gentle soothing touch feels good no matter who is doing it because the context doesn't matter; this touch means we are not abandoned. Studies have demonstrated that infants who were stroked smiled, vocalized more, and cried less than infants who were tickled or poked.[12] Infants preferred stroking to tickling and poking. Positive touch includes stroking, holding, hugging, kissing, hand-holding, and care giving. Lack of positive touch negatively affects growth, development, and emotional well-being. Conversely, soothing massage therapy with preterm infants enhanced weight gain. The areas of the body where massage was found to be most effective were the forehead, the scalp, the back of the head, the upper arms, and the hands.

Touch has meaning not just for humans but for other animals as well. Cats purr when petted. Dogs roll on their backs, I suspect, to get their tummies rubbed. All animals are quieter when held. Touch clearly gives pleasure, and it affects the stress axis. It is not just the individual who is touched that benefits; under most circumstances, the person who touches also benefits. See how good it feels to pet a dog.

There are many ways we touch in our culture. The most common is the handshake. The handshake has many meanings, from everything is all right, to we have a deal, to goodbye. The point is that touch bonds individuals. Its intent is contextual, but its meaning is personal; it creates an attachment. Shaking hands with an enemy is not done until peace is accepted on both sides. Comparisons between preschool-aged children in the United States and France revealed that French children were aggressive to their peers on playgrounds only 1% of the time, compared to 29% for American children. This finding correlated with the amount of time parents touched their children: the French, 35%, and the Americans, 11%.[13] Our current legal system in this country actively discourages unsolicited touch in this culture. It is impossible to determine what an individual's response is to someone else's touch, so we refrain from touching anybody.

Touch is reputed to have many healing qualities, and these have been organized into therapies. The most commonly used touch therapies include chiropractic, osteopath, cranial sacral therapies and acupressure, massage, Reiki, Rolfing, and so on. Some of these are discussed in more detail later. What is interesting is that when we touch and are touched, we experience sensations that are not directly assigned to the physical act. Even more remarkably, watching someone being touched can be relaxing.

What is the neurobiology of soothing touch? How does this soothing touch, what we call havening touch, produce a feeling of safety and allow us to escape from the inescapable? The technique that most resembles havening is Swedish massage. Swedish massage techniques include long strokes, kneading, friction, tapping, percussion, vibration, effleurage, and shaking motions:

Effleurage—Gliding strokes with the palms, thumbs, or fingertips.

Petrissage—Kneading movements with the hands, thumbs, or fingers.

Friction—Circular pressures with the palms of hands, thumbs, or fingers.

Vibration—Oscillatory movements that shake or vibrate the body.

Percussion—Brisk hacking or tapping.

Studies from the Touch Research Institute in Miami, Florida, have shown[14] that massage therapy enhances attentiveness, alleviates depressive symptoms, reduces pain, and improves immune function. Patients in the intensive care units of hospitals describe touch as critical to their feeling safe. There are measurable physiological changes associated with touch. Cortisol secretion, the stress hormone, is diminished with a soothing touch such as massage. There is an increase in dopamine (thought by some to also act as a reward chemical) and serotonin, as well as a decrease in norepinephrine, during massage. While these studies looked at peripheral concentrations of these chemicals, it is not unreasonable to assume that they are also altered centrally in the brain. If, as described earlier, depotentation occurs because of the production of a low frequency wave, is there a relationship between the neurochemicals released and the electrical activity in the brain? There is an abundance of data to support that serotonergic modulation of GABA neurons[15,18] and increased GABA release is associated with an increase in low-frequency (delta) waves in the amygdala.[16,17]

Can havening touch, the touch that tells us we are safe, be used to create a neurobiological equivalent of a haven, and also produce a depotentiating signal? If so, then we will have found a powerful method for treating a traumatization.

References

1. Aston-Jones, G., Akaoka, H., Charlety, P., and Chouvet, G. (1991). Serotonin selectively attenuates glutamate-evoked activation of noradrenergic locus coeruleus neurons. *J. Neurosci.* 11:760–769.
2. Baddeley, A. (1998). Recent developments in working memory. *Curr. Opin. Neurobiol.* 8:234–238.
3. Sarno, J. E. (2006). *The divided mind. The epidemic of mindbody disorders* (p. 159). New York, NY: Regan Books.
4. Callahan, R. (1981a). A rapid treatment for phobias. Collected papers of international college of applied kinesiology. (ICAK).
5. Shapiro, F. (Ed.)(2002). EMDR as an integrative psychotherapy approach. Washington, D.C.: American Psychological Association.
6. Levine, P. (1997). *Waking the tiger. Healing trauma.* Berkeley, CA: North Atlantic Books.
7. Levine, P. (1997). *Waking the tiger. Healing trauma* (p. 67). Berkeley, CA: North Atlantic Books.
8. Levine, P. (1997). *Waking the tiger. Healing trauma* (pp. 28–30). Berkeley, CA: North Atlantic Books.
9. Ogden, P., Minton, K., & Pain, C. (2006). *Trauma and the body. A sensorimotor approach to psychotherapy.* New York, NY: W.W. Norton & Co.
10. Van der Kolk, B. A., Weisaeth, L., & van der Hart, O. (2007). The history of trauma in psychiatry. In (Eds.), *Traumatic stress. The effects of overwhelming experience on mind, body and society.*

11. Hertenstein, M. J., Verkamp, J. M., Kerestes, A. M., & Holmes, R. M. (2006). The communicative functions of touch in humans, non-human primates, and rats: A review and synthesis of empirical research. *Genet. Soc. Psychol. Monogr.* 132:5–94.
12. Field, T., Diego, M., and Hernandez-Reif, M. (2005). Massage therapy research. *Dev. Rev.* 27:75–89.
13. Field, T. (1999). *American adolescents touch each other less and are more aggressive toward their peers as compared to French adolescents* [Statistical data included]. Retrieved from http://findarticles.com/p/articles/mi_m2248/is_136_34/ai_59810232/. Adolescence. Winter.
14. Field, T., Hernandez-Reif, M., Diego, M., Schanberg, S., & Kuhn, C. (2005). Cortisol decreases and serotonin and dopamine increase following massage therapy. *Int. J. Neurosci.* 115:1397–1413.
15. Ciranna, L. (2006). Serotonin as a modulator of glutamate- and GABA-mediated neurotransmission: Implications in physiological functions and pathology. *Curr. Neuropharmacol.* 4:101–114.
16. Halonen, T., Pitkanen, A., Koivisto, E., Partanen, J., & Riekkinen, P. J. (1992). Effect of vigabatrin on the electroencephalogram in rats. *Epilepsia* 33:122–127.
17. Gasanov, G. G., Melikov, E. M., & Ibrginov, R. Sh. (1981). Effect of serotonin injected into the amygdala on conditioned and unconditioned food reflexes and the EEG of cats. *Neurosci. Behav. Physiol.* 11(3): 207–212.
18. Stutzmann, G. E. & LeDoux, J. E. (1999). GABAergic antagonists block the inhibitory effects of serotonin in the lateral amyadala: A mechanism for modulation of sensory inputs related to fear conditoning. *J. Neurosci.* 19(11):RC8.

8

HAVENING

Havening involves imaginally activating the emotional or other component of a traumatized event. This is followed by application of havening touch, other sensory input, and a set of distracting tasks. If havening is successful, recall or reexperiencing of the traumatized component is altered or eliminated.

Havening can be considered to be a form of treatment grouped under the general term of exposure therapies. The most studied approach is called extinction training. Exposure of an animal to a neutral stimulus that is followed by an unconditional fear stimulus (UFS), such as a shock, conditions the animal to respond to the neutral stimulus with fear. Research attempting to eliminate the fear response to the neutral stimulus has shown that by exposing the animal to the neutral stimulus without the UFS, the animal will soon not respond to the neutral stimulus with fear. Credit for the discovery that reexposing the individual to a feared situation/object/memory could alter one's response to emotion-producing stimuli belongs to Wolpe,[1] in a therapy called counterconditioning or systematic desensitization. Here, the feared object was made less fearful by being presented in a safe surrounding. Both methods require exposure to a fear stimulus and both produce a diminution of fear responses. These approaches, however, do not remove the memory of the association, but merely provide a new learned response. While havening and extinction training require exposure to the emotion producing the fear, they produce fundamentally different results.

A New Approach

The use of touch after imaginal reexposure was first described by Dr. Roger Callahan. His seminal observation is recounted in his book *The Five-Minute Phobia Cure*.[2] Here, he reportedly had a woman who was thinking about her fear of water, tap herself under the eye. The phobia instantly disappeared. To explain this stunning result, he developed a theory based on acupuncture, energy fields, and meridians, very much an Eastern model. He calls his method Callahan Techniques–Thought Field Therapy (CT-TFT; see www.tftrx.com). It is grounded in traditional Chinese medicine, where the long-held belief is that energy courses through our body over certain well-defined pathways called meridians. If energy flows smoothly, we experience health and well-being. If, however, the energy is blocked from flowing, illness occurs. These meridians have special locations along their pathway called acupoints. These points are believed to regulate flow. Inserting needles or applying pressure at those locations restores healthy energy flow. According to Callahan, recalling a traumatic event creates a "thought field," an energy field that is perturbed because energy is blocked along the meridians. By having the individual tap an appropriate points in a specific order, healthy energy flow is restored, the pertubation removed, and the individual cured. In CT-TFT the points stimulated and the order in which they are stimulated depend on the problem to be solved. For example, phobias need points different from panic disorder, and different from chronic pain. In CT-TFT, tapping is combined with a Gamut procedure that includes a variety of distracting cognitive and eye movement processes and various mental tasks (Figures 8.1 and 8.2).

CT-TFT requires a person to "tune in to" the trauma and generate a **subjective unit of distress (SUD) score**.[1] SUD is a self-evaluated measure of the intensity of the recalled traumatic memory. The scale goes from 0 to 10, where 0 is no distress and 10 is extreme distress. The individual then taps 5 to 10 times on a set of predetermined points (see Figure 8.1) on the body, different points being used for different problems. After a round of tapping points, the individual taps on his hand at the Gamut spot, performing a Gamut procedure:

1. Close eyes
2. Open eyes
3. Point eyes down to left

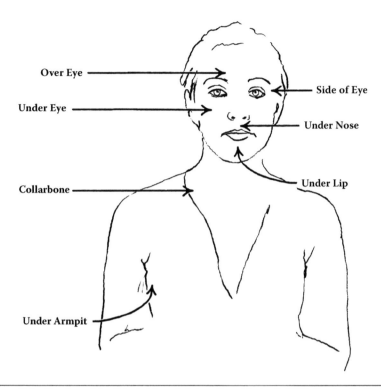

Figure 8.1 Tapping points. (Adapted from Callahan, R. and Trubo, R. 2002. *Tapping the Healer Within: Using Thought Field Therapy to Instantly Conquer Your Fears, Anxieties,* and *Emotional Distress.* New York: McGraw-Hill.)

4. Point eyes down to right
5. Big circle with eye
6. Big circle the other way
7. Hum "Happy Birthday"
8. Count to 5 aloud
9. Hum "Happy Birthday"

After several rounds of this tapping on points and the Gamut procedure, the problem resolves. The ready dismissal of CT-TFT by traditionally trained therapists can be appreciated. It makes no sense from a Western perspective. But Callahan's ideas struck a chord in other practitioners. Gary Craig, an engineer and student of Callahan, concluded that one set of points sufficed for all problems. He has

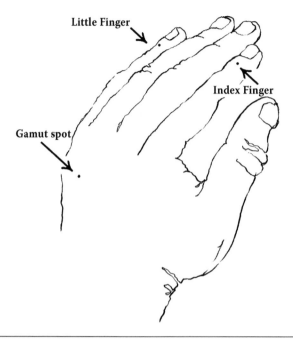

Figure 8.2 Gamut spot and hand-tapping points. (Adapted from Callahan, R. and Trubo, R. 2002. *Tapping the Healer Within: Using Thought Field Therapy to Instantly Conquer Your Fears, Anxieties,* and *Emotional Distress.* New York: McGraw-Hill.)

produced an important Web site for his version of Dr. Callahan's discovery and has named it Emotional Freedom Techniques (EFT) (see www.eftuniverse.com). Here, problems are activated by statements made by the patient and include affirmations such as "Even though I have this pain, I truly love and accept myself." His site has many clinical observations, suggestions for improving outcomes, and teaching DVDs. His biweekly newsletter describes successful case histories for a wide range of problems. He is well known for saying "Try it on everything." He claims EFT has fixed everything from broken toilets to the rash of poison ivy. The following interesting example was contributed to his web site.

Case Study
Arden Compton

Recently I took my family bowling. The bowling alley here in Brigham City was giving away a turkey to anyone who bowled three strikes in a row. So off we went to try our luck. Now, I am not a serious bowler; throughout my life, I have probably gone bowling about once a year ... maybe less. I usually bowl somewhere between 100 and 120. If I get over 120, it is a good game for me—if I get into the 130's—that's a really good game.

So getting three strikes in a row wasn't likely—I might get two or three strikes in a game, but not in a row. In my first frame, I knocked over eight pins, not bad. But I thought about how fun it would be to win a turkey and I decided to try some EFT. On my next turn, as I held the ball in my right hand, I tapped with my left hand on the face points and repeated in my mind, "This fear of not making a strike."

It took a little over five seconds to tap through that. This time I bowled a spare (meaning I knocked all the pins over in two tries), but was only one pin away from getting a strike. Each turn for the rest of the game, I went through the same tapping process. The next frame I bowled a strike! But on my next two frames I bowled a spare—I needed three strikes in a row.

I was feeling pretty good about my game at this point; I was on track to an above-average score for me. Then the next frame I bowled a strike, and the following frame I bowled another strike! At this point I did a little tapping before my next turn, there was a little pressure because I was going for the turkey on this one. I tapped on Fear of messing up the third strike ... fear of not getting a strike. I also tapped five seconds or so after I picked up my ball. And sure enough, I got a third strike!

I was so excited, I yelled loud enough for everyone in the bowling alley to hear me, "I won a turkey!" My wife and kids all gave me high fives. I ran over to the desk and had all the bowling alley employees give me a high five, there were some friends of mine several lanes down, and I ran over to them and had them give me high fives. So, the next time I got the ball I tapped again, and I got another strike! Four in a row! And then I got another strike, and another one, and another one! Seven strikes in a row by the time the game ended. I bowled a 236, 100 points beyond what I thought would be a really good game. Our friends even asked me to come bowl on their lane so I could help them win a turkey. On their lane, I bowled another strike.

However, I started having some uncertainty because I didn't think the bowling alley wanted me to win a turkey for other people—thus the next frame I ended the streak with a spare. I excused that by saying, "The ball slipped from my fingers," which it had, but I am almost certain it was because of those inner doubts about winning a turkey for someone else that I "sabotaged" it.

The statistical probability of me bowling eight strikes in a row has to be near zero. EFT really works! It calms us down, removes doubt and fear, which in turn allows us to perform at the level we are capable of. Not only can it help with bowling, but also every aspect of life—relationships, spirituality, money, professional goals, happiness & peace of mind, and the list could go on and on! EFT can help with so many things; it is awesome! When appropriate, try EFT for yourself and others—miracles can happen!

There are several other methods, all based on the idea of meridians, energy flow, and the use of acupoints and sensory input, such as tapping. These methods have led the Association for Comprehensive Energy Psychology (ACEP), an organization devoted to exploring various forms of bodily energetics, to adopt tapping on meridians as an important method of healing (for more information, see www.energypsych.org). As one might imagine, this therapy and its theoretical structure are considered controversial.

Andrade's Research

In the 1990s, Dr. Joaquin Andrade began organizing clinics in Uruguay to study this therapy. In the end over 29,000 patients were treated in 14 years. The results were remarkable.[3] For a wide range of problems, these methods were deemed successful in 76% of the subjects. By "successful," they were judged symptom free. This compares to 51% in the standard care group of cognitive behavioral therapy (CBT) and medication. The tapping procedure required a mean of 3 sessions, while the standard of care required a mean of 15 sessions. The patients were randomized, and the reviewers of the outcome were blinded as to what therapy was used. As close to a double-blind study as possible, the follow-up data included subjective scores after the termination of treatment by independent raters. The ratings, based on a scale of 1 to 5, estimated the effectiveness of the interventions as contrasted with other methods used (cognitive behavioral therapy or medications, or both). The numbers indicate that the rater believed that the tapping interventions produced:

1 = Much better results than expected with other methods
2 = Better results than expected with other methods

3 = Results similar to those expected with other methods

4 = Worse results than expected with other methods (only used in conjunction with other therapies)

5 = No clinical improvement at all or contraindicated

It must be emphasized that the following indications and contraindications are tentative guidelines based largely on the initial exploratory research and these informal assessments. In addition, the outcome studies have not been precisely replicated in other settings, and the degree to which the findings can be generalized is uncertain. Nonetheless, based upon the use of tapping techniques with a large and varied clinical population in 11 settings over a 14-year period, the following impressions can serve as a preliminary guide for selecting which clients are good candidates for acupoint tapping.

Rating of 1: Much Better Results Than With Other Methods

Many categories of anxiety disorders rated responded to tapping interventions much better than to other modalities. Among these are panic disorders with and without agoraphobia, agoraphobia without history of panic disorder, specific phobias, separation anxiety disorders, posttraumatic stress disorders, acute stress disorders, and mixed anxiety-depressive disorders. Also in this category were a variety of other emotional problems, including fear, grief, guilt, anger, shame, jealousy, rejection, painful memories, loneliness, frustration, love pain, and procrastination. Tapping techniques also seemed particularly effective with adjustment disorders, attention deficit disorders, elimination disorders, impulse control disorders, and problems related to abuse or neglect.

Rating of 2: Better Results Than With Other Methods

Although obsessive-compulsive disorders, generalized anxiety disorders, anxiety disorders due to general medical conditions, social phobias, and certain other specific phobias, such as a phobia of loud noises, were judged as not responding quite as well to energy interventions as other anxiety disorders, they still rated as being more responsive to an energy approach than to other methods. Also in this category were learning disorders, communication disorders, feeding and eating disorders of early childhood, tic disorders, selective mutism, reactive detachment disorders of infancy or early childhood, somatoform disorders, factitious disorders, sexual dysfunction, sleep disorders, and relational problems.

Rating of 3: Results Similar to Those Expected With Other Methods

Energy interventions seemed to fare equally well as other therapies commonly used for mild to moderate reactive depression, learning skills disorders, motor skills disorders, and Tourette's syndrome. Also in this category were substance abuse–related disorders, substance-induced anxiety disorders, and eating disorders. For these conditions, a number of treatment approaches can be effectively combined to draw upon the strengths of each.

Rating of 4: Worse Results Than Expected With Other Methods

The clinician's posttreatment ratings suggest that for major endogenous depression, personality disorders, and dissociative disorders, other therapies are superior as the primary treatment approach. Energy interventions might still be useful when used in an adjunctive manner.

Rating of 5: No Clinical Improvement or Contraindicated

The clinician's ratings of energy therapy with psychotic disorders, bipolar disorders, delirium, dementia, mental retardation, and chronic fatigue indicated no improvement.

Relapse rates, which mean a complete return of symptoms, were reported as 9% for the CBT/medication group and 4% for the tapping group.

Although this paper was criticized for lack of absolute rigor as to patient selection, assessment techniques, data analysis, and overall design, the sheer number of patients treated and the consistency of the results were intriguing.

These exposure therapies, CT-TFT, EFT, EMDR, and havening, all use an intervention immediately after reexposure. This time frame is critical for success. It is when the glutamate receptors are open and subject to disruption. The differences lie in the specific modes and frequency of touching, tapping, eye movements, or other sensory stimulation.

While all these approaches are successful, we believe that a neurobiological model allows us to understand this process and therefore to optimize therapy. Havening provides such a model.

Havening

Havening has three aspects:

1. Recall and activation of an emotional core
2. Distraction/other sensory input
3. Havening touch

The first is a process that recreates part or all of the traumatic encoding moment. This is followed by the simultaneous use of distraction and other sensory input to displace the component from working memory and havening touch to fool the brain into thinking a safe haven has been found. When successful, the individual is havened. Applying havening raises many questions that we have tried to answer.

- Why is it necessary to activate a component state before it can be treated?
- If an individual has a snake and elevator phobia, why do these problems need to be treated separately?
- Why does the same protocol work for different problems?
- What is the purpose of the touch/other sensory input and distraction?
- Why does the distress appear to diminish during the procedure?
- What is the transduction event that converts touch into a biological event in the brain?
- Why do patients feel calmer after treatment?
- Why and how do the memories become altered?
- Why does it produce a lasting effect?
- Why do some symptoms occasionally reoccur elsewhere?

To answer these questions, a recapitulation of what has been discussed is offered. Retrieval of a traumatized component by conscious or subconscious stimuli causes the release of the neurotransmitter glutamate in areas of the basolateral complex (BLC) corresponding to the specific neural circuit that initially encoded the traumatization.[4] It is by activating the pathway that the glutamate receptors become exposed and are susceptible to disruption.

Activation of the emotional component of the traumatized event→Working memory→Hippocampus→ BLC glutamate receptors activated→Distraction/sensory input/Havening touch→↑ Serotonin/ ↑ GABA/Low-frequency signal is generated→Depotentiation of activated BLC glutamate receptors→ ↓ Outflow from Amygdala→Emotional core de-linked from narrative→Traumatization cured

Havening causes the depotentiation of activated glutamate receptors and the de-linking of the emotional pathway in the BLC of the amygdala[5] (Figure 8.3). The Cortical→Context/Complex Content→ Recalled Event pathway sometimes remains intact (see Post-Havening), but without emotional amplification. (Figure 8.4).

Mechanism of Havening

Glutamate is the electricity that lights the event so it can be seen in the mind. Without the activation of glutamate receptors in the amygdala

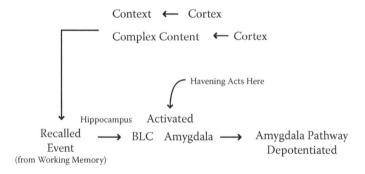

Figure 8.3   Havening disrupts amygdala activation and the emotional core is de-linked from the recalled event.

and the locus coeruleus, we are unable to permanently interrupt the pathway that allows us to reexperience the event. It can be speculated that each emotion and different circumstance has a specific and unique intra- and extra-amygdala pathway. Though feeling states can overlap, it is best to treat each emotion separately. The emotion of guilt should be treated separately from anger, and so on. On the other hand, if the stimulus uses the same pathway (e.g., fear of bridges), then removing the pathway that activates an emotion response for a generic bridge should suffice, although recalling the encoding event would be best. Because activation of glutamate receptors is common to all treatment approaches, the same protocol should work for all amygdala-based components. Decreasing distress from distraction during treatment results from diminished input to the amygdala from working memory. This inhibits outflow from the BLC to the Ce and diminishes NE outflow from the locus coeruleus. Unlike EMDR, where the client is asked to focus on the event, during havening, once the emotional component is activated, the client attends only to the instructions given by the therapist.

The pathways by which stimulation of peripheral mechanoreceptors in the skin produces a rise in serotonin and GABA and transduces a low-frequency signal remain unclear (see Appendix F). Havening touch produces a comforting sense, of feeling safe, not abandoned, and sleepiness. The low-frequency brain signal produced by havening, a delta wave, is seen in stage 3 sleep, the deepest, most restorative part of sleep. It would be impossible to reach stage 3 if there were any perceived threat. After havening, attempts at retrieval of the emotion generated by the memory are unsuccessful. The memory is no longer a traumatic memory; it no longer engages the amygdala (see "Post-havening" section below). If you have havened a symptom other than the emotional core, then it remains possible to reestablish a link to the original or related traumatic component. This is so because the amygdala-based emotional component has not been dissolved.

Successful havening removes the amygdala-activated traumatic emotion forever, and unless the exact moment of encoding is replicated, the ability of the traumatic components to activate the amygdala is lost forever. The process of depotentiation of the glutamate receptors

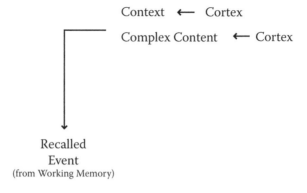

Figure 8.4 Post-havening without amygdala activation: Context and complex content no longer have emotional amplification.

in the amygdala has permanently altered the process of memory retrieval (Figure 8.4).

Since the havening has a hardwired soothing component, it should be possible to modulate and soothe everyday routine reflective emotions such as cravings, sadness, anger, and others. If not encoded as a trauma, why should this be so? The reason is the individual is emotionally activated and has an activated amygdala. Havening causes a rise in serotonin. This rise acts to decrease information flow and salience. It allows the working memory to let go of the stimulus. Of course, unlike removing a permanently encoded traumatic memory, once you stop havening, this feeling may return later.

Details of Havening

Recall and Activate the Emotional Core

If at all possible, the first task is to find and activate the event's emotional core. In many cases, multiple traumatic events have been encoded. This requires a thorough history, which, as treatment progresses, often unfolds in unpredictable ways. History taking is an ongoing process; it is really an inner-view, an internal view so to speak. We do this without intent to alter this view by talk; its purpose is to find the emotional core so that it can be havened. This is the fundamental difference between talk therapy and havening.

Janice's difficulty walking on uneven surfaces seemed odd. She carried a folding chair with her at all times so she could sit down as her feet became tired. She traces this problem to an event in the hospital when she had knee surgery and her legs were elevated and her feet not supported. For reasons that are not clear, she developed a bruise on the back of her leg, and from that time on she could not walk easily. After many sessions we were able to track numerous traumatizing events that could affect her perception of her feet. Havening events such as being held down in a dentist's chair with her feet dangling over the edge while having four wisdom teeth painfully extracted, watching a chicken being killed while its legs were held, walking on venetian blinds on the floor and cutting her foot, and having a nail stuck in her heel has yet to completely solve her problem. This lack of resolution suggests that earlier events have yet to be uncovered.

During the taking of a history it is important to inquire about the meaning of the event, previous landscapers (other life events that produce stress), and the individual's sense of inescapability about an event. Look for unconditioned fear stimuli, especially a sense of abandonment and unresolved anger (what we would call defensive rage). Ask if there was a prior injury to the area that now has chronic pain. Ask if there were any unresolved childhood memories that still produce distress today. Ask if there were any motor vehicle accidents, or whether he or she recalls when the problem first started. Follow trails and observe physiological responses to statements and memories. Be prepared to ask difficult questions, but don't press for answers. Search dreams. After a thorough history, the therapist must decide whether the behavior or the feelings he or she observes are consequences of a traumatization. As mentioned earlier, traumatization can occur even with what appears to be a trivial incident if it has meaning to the individual.

A good therapeutic relationship is critical to tease out these areas so they can be addressed. The clues, the dead ends, and the lack of progress are all part of the process that eventually leads to a cure. This seems to be particularly true in the case of chronic pain and posttraumatic stress disorder (PTSD), where the memories remain unavailable or are dissociated and one might think that havening hasn't worked. Gary Craig, the originator of EFT, describes many ideas for getting around what seems like failure (www.eftuniverse.com). There is much that can be learned as one uses this approach, and using the model described here, your skills will improve over time.

If one cannot readily find the emotional core, focusing on a distressing symptom is often useful. Simply activate the distress surrounding the symptom. Be as specific as possible when describing the symptom (e.g., the right side of the upper back or neck) prior to havening (see Appendix E).

Havening sometimes produces the most remarkable of medical miracles, an instantaneous cure. Observing this process seems to belie the statement that seeing is believing. Surely a trick has been played and the long-term emotional problems, the pain, the fear will most certainly return. Most patients are in disbelief. More often, only a part of the underlying emotional issues is resolved during any single treatment session. This is true because traumatization begets traumatization, so that removal of one event uncovers others.

Distraction and Other Sensory Input

The therapeutic component of the havening process requires that both distraction and other sensory input and havening touch be performed immediately after activation. We use a relatively standard sequence, but the therapist can use what he or she thinks works best for the patient. Future research will look at different tasks to optimize distraction and comforting. The client and I are comfortably seated facing each other so our eyes are pretty much aligned. I then give him or her a brief set of instructions:

1. Once we start, I want you just to listen to the sound of my voice as I tell you what I need you to do.
2. After bringing the event/symptom to consciousness and stating an SUD score, it is important to keep your mind focused on the tasks at hand.
3. During the session I request that you not speak spontaneously.
4. In between havening rounds, I want your eyes to remain closed and for you to stare at the back of your eyelids.
5. If for any reason you begin to feel uncomfortable, let me know.

After recall of a traumatic component with their eyes closed, an SUD score is obtained from the client. I start with tapping on the collarbone with both hands on both sides; it has a nice vibratory sense to it. While I am doing this, I have the client open their eyes, look down to the left, down to the right, and make a big circle, first one way and then the other. I have them close their eyes and count slowly (one number per second) from 1 to 20 aloud as they visually imagines walking up a flight of stairs, one number for each step. I instruct them as follows: "As you walk up the stairs, each step causes you to feel more relaxed, and when you reach the top, a beautiful vista awaits you." This activates the visual-spatial (imagining walking up stairs) component of working memory. I then have them hum a tune to activate the phonological component of working memory. The cycle of visual-spatial and phonological distraction along with various touch techniques is repeated with different stimuli. Different tasks, for example, visualizing shooting basketballs, throwing horseshoes, climbing stairs, or rowing a boat, and different tunes, for example, "Mary Had a Little Lamb," "Take Me Out to the Ball Game," and so on, are used with each round. Several rounds are repeated until the SUD score either reaches 0 or cannot be lowered further. Finally, I have the client open their eyes and have them follow my hand to the four corners of the visual field. I ask them to close their eyes, take a deep breath, then say OMMMMM while exhaling. I suggest the client should lower their shoulders as I stroke from their shoulders down to their hands. I then obtain another SUD score.

Havening Touch

Touch is among the most powerful forms of communication. Havening touch is meant to be comforting, soothing, relaxing, and unhurried. It is not a light touch, nor is it heavy handed. Some of the areas that are touched are shown in Figures 8.5 to 8.8. I generally vary the areas of touch during each cycle.

During this process I use an unmodulated, somewhat monotonous voice that is never hurried. I am always encouraging. Phrases in the same unmodulated tone, such as "almost home" and "you are

Figure 8.5   Face havening. (Courtesy of Ronald Ruden and Steve Lampasona.)

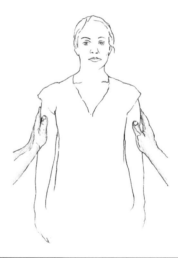

Figure 8.6   Arm havening. (Courtesy of Ronald Ruden and Steve Lampasona.)

excellent at this," are interjected while comforting and soothing by havening touch. Rarely does this process take more than 10 minutes, and for most, an SUD score of 0 is reached. If an SUD of 0 is not reached, I take a further history to look for earlier clues. As I begin

Figure 8.7   Hug havening. (Courtesy of Ronald Ruden and Steve Lampasona.)

Figure 8.8   Forehead havening. (Courtesy of Ronald Ruden and Steve Lampasona.)

to explore the emotional and physical effects of traumatization, I am often struck by how many emotional issues an event can produce. For example, individuals who have been sexually abused in their youth experience anger, shame, and guilt. Each of these emotions must be treated separately. In addition, sometimes the anger is also directed at the parent who allowed the abuse to occur. People with back pain secondary to an accident need to have not only the accident havened but also the fear of recurrence of the pain. The more specific one can be, the more likely havening will be successful. One might be afraid of snakes, but it is the slithering aspect that makes the patient's skin get goose bumps and activates the amygdala. Kinesthetic aspects, involving movement, are very important.

Havening: A Summary

After obtaining a history, have the client activate an emotional core of the traumatic event. This is the most critical aspect of the therapy, and time spent here is well rewarded. If this is not possible, have the client focus on their most troublesome symptoms. At the outset of event activation, I encourage them to make a movie of the event as bright and detailed as possible. I occasionally aid him or her in his or her visualization. Generally no more than 30 seconds is given before I request that they provide an SUD score. After an SUD score is obtained:

1. *Instruct them not to think about the event or component again.*
2. *While tapping on the client's collarbone, have the client open their eyes and look down to the left, then right, and then make a circle with his or her eyes in both directions.*
3. *Instruct the client to once again close their eyes and imaginally perform a distracting visual process (walking up a flight of stairs while counting aloud from 1 to 20 for 20 steps). This is performed while the therapist applies arm havening.*
4. *After the count reaches 20 have the client hum a song with his or her eyes closed (e.g., "Take Me Out to the Ball Game," "Happy Birthday," "Old McDonald Had a Farm," etc.). Arm havening is continued. After completion of the song, have the client open his or her eyes and follow your finger for one sequence: up, down, to both sides, then up again.*
5. *Have the client take a deep breath and exhale with an OMMMMM; move your hand downward as they close their eyes.*
6. *Ask them to lower their shoulders and continue arm havening.*
7. *Ask them to close their eyes, look at the back of their eyelids, and only listen to your voice. Obtain an SUD score.*
8. *Repeat processes 1 to 7 using different havening touch methods and distractions until the SUD is 0 or remains fixed after three rounds.*

I have found great difficulty in treating trauma with havening if a severe anxiety disorder (i.e., obsessive compulsive disorder) is also present.

Self-Havening

Havening can be self-applied for many routine emotional states. However, for reactive and reflective emotions that are traumatically based, it is best to have a therapist involved. There are many subtleties involved with using this approach, and guidance by an experienced practitioner is helpful.

Self-havening may be a useful approach to disorders involving obsessional thinking and repetitive behaviors. Thus, as described by Dr. David Lake (see p. 185), this works for compulsive disorders such as bulimia, checking, hand washing, and hair pulling. It is best not to fight the desire to perform the action. Rather, view the desire as an activation of the BLC and apply havening at that moment. Over time, a person should be able to control or eliminate the unwanted behavior. In addition, for those who struggle with panic disorder, assume the attack is an activation of the BLC and apply self-havening. Try not to understand why it is happening or attempt to will it away. Diagrams of self-havening methods are shown in Figures 8.9 to 8.10.

Self-havening can be done in the presence of a therapist. However, unless the client is touch averse (see Appendix G), I believe that the

Figure 8.9 One way of face self-havening. (Courtesy of Ronald Ruden and Steve Lampasona.)

Figure 8.10   One way of face self-havening. (Courtesy of Ronald Ruden and Steve Lampasona.)

therapist should touch the patient, as the difference between self-touch and a therapist's touch may be significant.

Post-Havening

A relaxed state is always seen after successful havening, and retrieval of the memory is altered in one of four ways:

1. The memory is blocked and is inaccessible.
2. The memory is fuzzy and incomplete.
3. The memory is viewed from a distance and as a detached observer.
4. The memory is richer in peripheral detail, but the fearful component is less clear or absent.

These four outcomes are directly related to the loss of norepinephrine, depotentiation of the BLC pathway, and the subsequent elimination of the emotional response (see Figure 8.4). Recall of the fearful component of the memory is immediately impaired and further diminishes over time. Thus, when recalling an event after successful havening, it appears distant; a few minutes later it will appear more distant.

Figure 8.11 Self-havening hug. (Courtesy of Ronald Ruden and Steve Lampasona.)

The component parts are no longer linked because the UFS/unimodal sensory content association that led to an emotional response has been disrupted. The removal of the emotional component detaches us, and we view the event dispassionately. Finally, if the feared object is eliminated, the context of the event that had been overshadowed may now become available. For example, for a traumatized memory, prior to havening, we selectively remember the emotionally rich component of a memory at the expense of other aspects of the memory of the event. In this moment of fear we often narrow our focus to the fearful object. We recall the gun, the knife, but not necessarily the surroundings; they are not readily accessible to conscious recall because our main focus is the feared object. If the feared component is eliminated, the context can be recalled.

Fannie remembers that the door was open when her cousin told of her father being killed in a motorcycle accident. It was only after havening that she remembered her cousin was wearing pink pants.

It is useful to debrief the client by asking him or her to see if he or she can recall the memory and tell how it appears to him or her. Both the therapist and the client will learn from this question. The mind solves the problems in sometimes remarkable ways. The most common solution is metaphor.

Diana was having panic attacks. She was extremely stressed at work, and most of her panic came from her job in the kitchenware department of a large store. Her boss was out of control, micromanaging everyone without any sense of what he was saying. At the outset she saw herself walking on the floor where she worked. Seeing all the employees and her boss, she developed an SUD score of 7–8. After havening she was asked to revisit the floor in her imagination and found, much to her surprise, that the floor was empty of people.

If recalling the event still produces an emotional response, repeating the process is helpful. This is also a call to seek other aspects of the event or previous events that need havening.

Postscript

In the final analysis, traumatization produces a state different from those produced by other stressors. It is permanent unless treated. It is likely we all suffer with some traumatization from events in our lives. Some of us are greatly affected; others are affected in minor ways. Indeed, depending on other factors, sometimes traumatization motivates us to be better than we would have been without the experience. Some patients feel that removing these memories will change them and they wish to keep whatever the emotional state is alive within (see Appendix H). Nonetheless, for most, traumatization produces a never-ending distress.

To use these techniques, to become a healer, even if you just want to self-heal, you must be willing to become an explorer. Explore what comforts you, explore what makes you uncomfortable, bravely seek the emotional core of the problem, and then create a haven.

References

1. Wolpe, J. (1958). *Psychotherapy by reciprocal inhibition.* Stanford, CA: Stanford University Press.
2. Callahan, R. (1993). *The five-minute phobia cure.* Wilmington, DE: Enterprise.
3. Andrade, J., & Feinstein, D. (2003). *Preliminary report on the first large scale study of energy psychology.* Retrieved from www.emofree.com/research/andradepaper.htm
4. Rainnie, D. G., Mania, I., Mascagni, F., & Shinnick-Gallaher, P. (1991). Excitatory transmission in the basolateral amygdala. *J. Neurophysiol.* 66:986–998.
5. Kim, J., Lee, S., Park, K., Hong, I., Song, B., Son, G., Park, H., Kim, W. R., Park, E., Choe, H. K., Lee, C., Sun, W., Kim, K., Shin, K. S., & Choi, S. (2007). Amygdala depotentiation and fear exinction. *Proceedings of the National Academy of Sciences.* (104) 52: 20955–20960.

A Brief Introduction to Psychosensory Therapies

Extrasensory Responses

While this book focuses on havening, a psychosensory therapy that employs touch, other sensory stimuli can produce extrasensory responses as well. Like touch, extrasensory responses to sound, taste, smell, and sight can be exciting or calming and can be innate or learned. For all living animals, predator and prey alike, the existence of extrasensory responses suggests that they are useful for survival.

We defined extrasensory responses earlier as those that arise unbidden from sensory input. One of the most remarkable journeys evolving from an extrasensory response is described in Proust's volumes *Remembrance of Things Past*.[1] In these volumes Proust describes his journey to uncover the source of an event that startled him. It illustrates how a sensory cue can bring back memory and emotion. Clearly, the sensory input itself is not the cause of the response; if anyone else drank the tea and ate the cake, their reaction would be quite different. The response is a consequence of subconscious associations. His description is important because it reveals that in addition to the negatively valenced traumatic memories, positively valenced memories can also be recalled when suitably stimulated:

> Many years had elapsed during which nothing of Combray, save what
> was comprised in the theatre and the drama of my going to bed there,
> had any existence for me, when one day in winter, as I came home, my
> mother, seeing that I was cold, offered me some tea, a thing I did not
> ordinarily take. I declined at first, and then, for no particular reason,
> changed my mind. She sent out for one of those short, plump little cakes

called "petites madeleines," which look as though they had been moulded in the fluted scallop of a pilgrim's shell. And soon, mechanically, weary after a dull day with the prospect of a depressing morrow, I raised to my lips a spoonful of the tea in which I had soaked a morsel of the cake. No sooner had the warm liquid, and the crumbs with it, touched my palate, a shudder ran through my whole body, and I stopped, intent upon the extraordinary changes that were taking place. An exquisite pleasure had invaded my senses, but individual, detached, with no suggestion of its origin. And at once the vicissitudes of life had become indifferent to me, its disasters innocuous, its brevity illusory—this new sensation having had on me the effect which love has of filling me with a precious essence; or rather this essence was not in me, it was myself. I had ceased now to feel mediocre, accidental, mortal. Whence could it have come to me, this all-powerful joy? I was conscious that it was connected with the taste of tea and cake, but that it infinitely transcended those savours, could not, indeed, be of the same nature as theirs. Whence did it come? What did it signify? How could I seize upon and define it?

I drink a second mouthful, in which I find nothing more than in the first, a third, which gives me rather less than the second. It is time to stop; the potion is losing its magic. It is plain that the object of my quest, the truth, lies not in the cup but in myself. The tea has called up in me, but does not itself understand, and can only repeat indefinitely with a gradual loss of strength, the same testimony; which I, too, cannot interpret, though I hope at least to be able to call upon the tea for it again and to find it there presently, intact and at my disposal, for my final enlightenment. I put down my cup and examine my own mind. It is for it to discover the truth. But how? What an abyss of uncertainty whenever the mind feels that some part of it has strayed beyond its own borders; when it, the seeker, is at once the dark region through which it must go seeking, where all its equipment will avail it nothing. Seek? More than that: create. It is face to face with something, which does not so far exist, to which it alone can give reality and substance, which it alone can bring into the light of day.

There are two pathways that produce extrasensory responses useful for healing. The first is an intrinsic pathway that travels from the receptors in the sense organs to the brain and directly affects neuro-chemical release. The second pathway involves a learned response.

Intrinsic and Conditioned Extrasensory Responses

The response to a threatening stimulus that produces fear is not enough to ensure survival. We also need to feel comfortable, so that we can laugh, eat leisurely, mate, and not experience a sense of urgency from chronic vigilance. Thus, there needs to be stimuli that indicate safety, that we are not the current object of someone's appetite. Perception of safety decreases processing of information about the world around us; vigilance is diminished. All psychosensory therapies rely on this fact; the extrasensory response must make us feel that the world is a safe haven. This is experienced and observed in herding animals, as discussed earlier. This feeling allowed mammal mothers to care for their young and produce a bond that allowed for exploration. Are there stimuli that can do this naturally without learning? The answer is yes. Breathing quietly while sitting in the posture of cupped hands in your lap, dropped shoulders, and slack jaw helps soothe anger and alleviate anxiety (see Figure 9.1 and give it a try). The smell of lavender makes us less anxious. Order makes us feel more secure. Havening, touch in a therapeutic setting, makes us feel calm. These feelings arise from intrinsic pathways, hardwired at birth, that make us feel safe.

The other source of a healing extrasensory experience is a conditioned response that has been paired with a sensory stimulus, for example, the smell of chicken soup (like homemade) or the sound of familiar folk music (like home). In general, home is considered a haven.

Psychosensory Therapy

There are two fundamental types of psychosensory therapy: One is nonspecific and causes a global reduction in stress responsiveness. This type of therapy increases resilience. This leads to an overall increase in the threshold to further traumatization. The other therapy type is event specific. (A partial list of these therapies can be found on p. 6.)

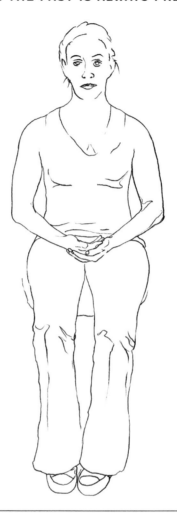

Figure 9.1　Picture of posture. (Courtesy of Ronald Ruden and Steve Lampasona.)

Nonspecific Psychosensory Therapies

There are many body (somatic, visceral, brain)-mind systems that appear to alter neurochemical concentrations and activities. They are nonspecific therapies that provide temporary changes in our landscape. The time course for therapeutic effect varies, but when a nonspecific psychosensory therapy is applied at appropriate intervals, long-standing changes may occur. These therapies are truly body → mind, where sensory input affects brain → mind functioning.

Touch

Touch, as we think about it, is based on mechanoreceptors of no emotional importance embedded in the skin. These mechanoreceptors monitor the perception of pain, heat, temperature, pressure, vibration, and position. Indeed, from a Western medical perspective, there is no expectation that touch should treat or heal anything. Nonetheless, its effect must exert some evolutionary advantage. We speculate that gentle, soothing touch produces the feeling that you are not alone and defenseless, you are not abandoned.

Acupuncture, part of the 4,000-year-old practice in **traditional Chinese medicine** (TCM), has no intrinsic emotional value, yet the insertion of needles or the applying of pressure along acupoints has powerful effects on mood and pain. There is extensive research demonstrating a rise of serotonin and opioid-like substances, increasing comfort and a sense of well-being, with acupuncture needling.[2]

Reiki[3] is a Japanese touch technique for stress reduction and relaxation that also promotes healing by its effect of the laying on of hands or merely moving the hands over the body. Its effect is nonspecific. Reiki is based on the idea that an unseen "life force energy" flows through us, causing us to be alive. If one's life force energy is low, then one is more likely to get sick or feel stress. If it is high, one is more capable of being happy and healthy. The word *Reiki* is made of two Japanese words: *Rei*, which means "God's wisdom or the higher power," and *Ki*, which is "life force energy." So Reiki is actually "spiritually guided life force energy."

Touch as in massage therapy and Rolfing[4] (a form of deep massage) reputedly breaks down tissue tensions and restores normal lengths to the muscles and tendons, thus reducing stress. As mentioned earlier, massage has been shown to cause a rise in serotonin and dopamine as well as a decrease in cortisol.

There are many therapeutic modalities that have evolved using touch to heal. Therapeutic touch[5] is a contemporary healing modality drawn from ancient practices and developed by Dora Kunz and Dolores Krieger. Callahan Techniques–Thought Field Therapy (CT-TFT) and Emotional Freedom Techniques (EFT) and many of the touch therapies mentioned above are based on the assumption that all beings are composed of complex fields of energy, and that altering the flow of energy through these fields enhances healing. While evidence to support this assumption is lacking, these therapies can produce amazing results.

Posture (Position Sense)/Kinesthetic

Position and facial expressions are another form of nonspecific psycho-sensory therapy. Take a relaxed posture and see how that affects you. Yoga[6] is an extraordinary psychosensory therapy. There is no Western explanation as to why sensing the breath and various body positions should produce calmness, increase resilience to stress, and diminish compulsive behavior. Yet they appear to do so. One explanation is that when we are anxious or stressed—both common problems in today's world—we tend to breathe in a more shallow way. Encountering a predator causes us to breathe through our mouths rapidly. We do not breathe through our nose when being chased because we can move more air through our mouths. We speculate that nasal breathing naturally slows our breath and that feeds back to the brain that a predator is not pursuing us and we are safe. There are many types of yoga, from simple breathing and posture (Hatha) yoga, to hot (Bikram) yoga, to power (Astanga) yoga. These forms of yoga provide multiple sensory inputs that align with how the individual experiences the world. As described above, using kinesthetic and breathing techniques, a simple method to calm an agitated individual is to have him or her sit in a chair with feet flat on the floor, hands cupped upward in the lap, shoulders down, and jaw slack, and breath through the nose slowly (see p. 122). This posture is the physical opposite of defensive rage. It is almost impossible to remain agitated. Interestingly, smiling[7] can act as a psychosensory therapy. Try smiling whenever you can; even an upward lips motion can have beneficial effects over the course of time. Frowning can have the opposite effect.

Vision

The Chinese describe the use of feng shui,[8] the arrangement of visual stimuli to induce serenity, in homes and gardens. This is so because background patterns that are orderly facilitate the identification of a predator. Disorder makes it likely that a predator can hide more readily. Feng shui places the person in positions such that he or she sees the world. Thus, beds and desks face the door. The ability to detect disorder and the positioning of our visual line of sight to provide the widest field serve, in a very primitive way, to protect us.

Sunsets, beautiful vistas, and grand canyons provide calm. Beauty, as in the eye of the beholder, can engender good feelings. Certainly a smiling symmetric face attracts attention and makes us feel happier. Interestingly, individuals witnessing the havening process also experience comfort and well-being. This response is similar to a phenomenon called surrogate tapping,[9] where, after reactivation of a traumatic component, the therapist taps on his or her own body and the client receives a benefit. This response is probably mediated via mirror neurons (see Appendix A). The exploration of this extraordinary extrasensory effect is just beginning.

The lack of sunlight during the winter months leads to depression,[10] increased risk for suicide, and substance abuse. Adding light has produced documented results for disorders such as seasonal affective disorder.

Sound

Music and sound were thought by the ancient Greeks to penetrate into the depths of the soul. Music reportedly can soothe a savage beast. The sound of falling water is calming. Speed, rhythm, instrumentation, melody, and minor versus major keys are some aspects of music that affect us. Early forms of music used chanting. While chanting has no set rhythm, it is the types of sounds used and the ability to sustain a breath that determine the nature of the chant. Religious ceremonies use communal chanting to achieve a feeling of safety and unity.

It is hard for a Western ear not to get excited during the last few moments of Beethoven's Ninth Symphony or feel calmed by his Moonlight Sonata. Some have claimed that Mozart's music is therapeutic. Popular music moves us to dance, sing, and experience happiness. While music won't make us smarter, it will increase our ability to solve certain problems, probably by nonspecific changes in our mood and arousal. Some researchers feel that music exerts its calming affect by inhibiting other sensory input from impacting on the senses. Many find that music sets a mood. Seasonal music tends to make us more cheerful, while gentle music makes us feel romantic.[11]

W. B. Canon[12] discusses other aspects of psychosensory observations, such as the effect of martial music on fighting. "For the grim purposes of war, the reed and the lute are grotesquely ill-suited; to rouse men to action strident brass and the jarring instruments of percussion are used in full force.... The Romans charged their foes amid the blasts of trumpets and horns ... the Russian General Linevitch is quoted as saying 'Music is one of the most vital ammunitions of the army.'"

Taste and Smell

Taste is another sense that has effects other than taking away hunger. Best defined by what is called comfort foods,[13] these foods generally have a high carbohydrate or sugar content. Sugar seems to be the most consistent mind-altering substance and is very often craved. This may be the result of the sugar in mother's milk when we are born. Other foods are culturally based, similar to music, ranging from chicken soup to baklava to chocolate pudding. They are associated with good feelings and home and safety. Because of the extrasensory component of food, we sometimes incorrectly use it as a drug to remove anxiety and take away boredom, leading to serious consequences in terms of obesity.

Aromatherapy[14] shows modest but significant effects in a variety of situations. In one study, researchers studied lavender, rose, and lemon essential oils for their antistress action. Somewhat surprisingly, lemon oils were the best antistress aromas for the stress-producing situations tested.

Thus, sight, sound, smell, taste, touch, and position, and probably temperature and humidity and other environmental stimuli (low barometric pressure has been associated with increased violence[15]), have been studied, and some appear to have a beneficial effect. The mechanism by which these non-emotional sensory inputs act to alter our feelings needs further clarification. It is possible there remain undiscovered sensors in our bodies that transduce environmental sensations into affecting how we feel and act. How and why these inputs affect us, both for the long and the short term, will be the subject of future research.

Event-Specific Psychosensory Therapies

In the animal model, exposure therapy is called extinction training. This procedure takes an animal conditioned to produce a fear response to a sound (CS) that previously predicted a shock (an unconditioned fear stimulus, UFS) and then does not shock the animal (CS → //UFS). After several trials the animal learns a new response to the CS, no shock (CS → No Shock). Research has shown that the original CS → UFS → Fear pathway, however, is not extinguished and can be readily reinstated. This is different than what is seen after successful havening. Here, the ability to reinstate the emotional response is eliminated. The different outcomes between extinction training (non-reinforced exposure to the CS) versus psychosensory therapy (comforting touch and distraction after imaginal exposure) suggest that a different mechanism is at work. Indeed, it can be suggested that unlike extinction training, no new learning takes place in havening, just the elimination of the relationship between the event and the emotion.

Another interesting question arises: Can we use this process in reverse, that is, associate a sensory process with an emotion and use it for good? One approach to a conditioned psychosensory healing is called anchoring. It relates a sense of touch to a craving. The process is simple. For example, the individual thinks of something he or she craves, let's say chocolate. They are then instructed to make it disgusting. Imagine eating hair and dust-covered chocolate. Simultaneously, he or she squeezes the thumb and the middle finger of the right hand. This process associates the physical act of squeezing with the now disgusting craved object. Second, the individual now thinks of something pleasurable and squeezes the thumb and middle finger of the other hand. When craving for chocolate occurs, a combination of squeezing the thumb and forefinger of the right hand followed by squeezing the left eliminates the craving.

Psychosensory therapy as a general field has been studied in a fragmented way. There are probably common mechanisms by which these senses affect us. Further research will allow us to understand how to use these powerful, safe techniques to treat trauma-based disorders and increase resilience.

References

1. Proust, M. (1919–1927). *Remembrance of things past: Swan's way: Within a budding grove* (Definitive French Pleiade ed., C. K. S. Moncrieff & T. Kilmartin, Trans., Vol. 1, pp. 48–51). New York, NY: Vintage.
2. Cabioglu, M. T., & Surucu, H. S. (2009). Acupuncture and neurophysiology. *Med. Acupuncture* 21:13–20.
3. The Reiki Center. Retrieved December 10, 2008, from http://www.reiki.com. See this site and www.reiki.org for more information.
4. European Rolfing Association. Retrieved December 10, 2008, from http://www.rolfing.org. See this site for more information, as well as the following:
   Field, T., Hernandez-Reif, M., Diego, M., Schanberg, S., & Kuhn, C. (2005). Cortisol decreases and serotonin and dopamine increase following massage therapy. *Int. J. Neurosci.* 115:1397–1413.
   Field, T., Diego, M., & Hernandez-Reif, M. (2005). Massage therapy research. *Dev. Rev.* 27:75–89.
5. Therapeutic Touch. Retrieved December 10, 2008, from http://www.therapeutictouch.org
6. Yang, K. (2007). A review of yoga programs for the four leading risk factors of chronic disease. *Evid. Based Complem. Alt. Med.* 4:487–491.
   Cloud, J. (2009, January 16). How to lift your mood? Try smiling. *Time.* Retrieved from http://www.time.com/time/health/0,8599,1871687,00.html/
7. Matsumoto, D., & Willingham, R. (2009). Spontaneous facial expressions of emotion in congenitally and non-congenitally blind individuals. *J. Personality Soc. Psychol.* 96:1–10.
8. Wikipedia. *Feng shui.* Retrieved December 10, 2008, from http://en.wikipedia.org/wiki/
9. Kurczak, R. *How to do intentional (or surrogate) EFT. A four part series.* Retrieved January 12, 2010, from http://emofree.com/Articles2/International-tapping-series.htm
10. *Seasonal affective disorder.* Retrieved December 19, 2008, from http://www.nlm.nih.gov/medlineplus.seasonalaffectivedisorder.htm/
11. *Music therapy.* Retrieved December 19, 2008, from http://www.nccata.org/music_therapy.htm/
12. Canon, W. B. (1929). *Bodily changes in pain, hunger, fear and rage.* New York, NY: Harper Torchbooks.

13. Wikipedia. *Comfort food.* Retrieved December 19, 2008, from http://en.wikipedia/wiki/Comfort_Food/

14. Fellows, D., Barnes, K., & Wilkinson, S. (2004). Aromatherapy and massage for symptom relief in patients with cancer. *Cochrane Database Syst. Rev.* 2:CD00287.

15. Schory, T. J., Piecznaki, N., Nair, S., & el-Mallakh, R. S. (2003). Barometric pressure, emergency psychiatric visits and violent acts. *Can. J. Psychiatry* 48:624–627.

10
TRAUMA STORIES AND TRAUMA CURES

Patients wrote the material in this chapter after undergoing havening and gave permission for their stories to be told. They are presented without discussion and are meant to illustrate the myriad of treatable problems that can arise from traumatization. It is hoped that these patients' stories will encourage a search for a traumatic origin for puzzling problems.

Loss of a Loved One

In the story of the widow in Chapter 5, we chose to haven the terror of the initial phone call: the anger and frustration about traveling to the hospital and the look given by the doctor.

> There are not enough words that will express the deep gratitude I have for this amazing peace and calmness that has returned to my entire being. Last night, when I left your office, I felt so euphoric and calmed. I said to Arnold you must have drugged me in some way. I even thought perhaps there was something on your hand every time you touched my face and I took a deep breath. I am just amazed and totally blown away by this instantaneous freedom from the horrific prison I was in for three years.
>
> When we left your office, we went across the street to the parking garage and an alarm and flashing went off. I never even flinched; normally I would have what I used to call "a squirt," which I believe was a release of cortisol from the pit of my stomach, and it would have made me feel extremely anxious and vigilant. I had nothing of the sort, I heard it, but did not feel it. The same with driving home, stuck in NYC traffic for at least two hours. I had to tell Arnold to

calm down, that it was okay, it was only traffic—it didn't bother me in the least. Had I not had your treatment, I would have been raging, swearing, and very angry. I am so amazed! On the drive home today, I heard ambulances and sirens and exactly that: I heard it but did not feel it! When I try to recall the events, they are jumbled, but I no longer feel them. So far my experience after day 1 is I can hear things and see them, but no longer experience them physically or in any sort of uncomfortable way. You gave me back my peace; I am ever so grateful and pray that it lasts.

Three days later she writes: "I really am going to be okay."

Loss of a Loved One

I was particularly haunted by the image of my father in the hospital right after he died. I dreamt about the image, and the mere thought of it would bring tears to my eyes. I willingly participated in the havening exercise. I am happy to say the vividness of the image has faded, and while I do picture it sometimes, it is not a frequent guest of my dreams and no longer elicits a strong emotion. It frankly never occurred to me I was suffering from a posttraumatic syndrome. I can't remember the purpose of the visit that day, but I do know that it has given me many nights of peace.

September 11, 2001

Since September 11, 2001, I suffered extreme anxiety and have had difficulty sleeping. Each night I would lie awake, watching airplanes fly up the Hudson River through my bedroom window. Each time one took a flight path I thought to be too low, I would jump out of bed, scurry to my living room, and watch the plane, waiting to see if I needed to wake my family for a quick exit. I thought for sure one of these planes would eventually come straight for my building. I visualized it happening and lived that dreadful moment over and over in my mind.

While my difficulty with 9/11 was not as severe as many others', things just hadn't been the same. I never sought professional help because I felt that countless hours of therapy would be fruitless, depleting not my anxieties and stress but my wallet. When you offered to help, I didn't fully understand just what an effect that dreadful day had on me. Nor did I imagine how much life was about to change.

I am not sure I understand your treatment or its scientific explanation, but you stopped the airplanes. Not only did you stop the planes from coming, but also you changed my life in a very big way. You probably saw it in my countenance after your treatment. I felt as though a tremendous burden was lifted. After leaving your office, I went home, saw my beautiful wife and adorable daughter, spent a lovely evening in their company, went to bed at 11, and had the best night sleep since 9/10. The planes never came.

For the first time since that day, I can say that I am truly happy. I don't know if I am being naïve thinking my family and I are now safe, but it doesn't really matter. What matters is that I am now enjoying life again to its fullest extent.

Medical Trauma

Thank you again for the havening. My breast cancer diagnosis was hitting me hard, and while I was physically fine, I could not get the last appointment with my surgeon out of my mind. All I thought of was a reoccurrence. My moods varied between anxious and depressed. I spent the weekend in bed just crying. I actually called into work sick the Friday before I saw you because my eyes were swollen shut from crying.

When I came to see you my blood pressure was 150/100. My heart felt like it was going to beat right through my chest. When you asked me to visualize the doctor's appointment, I started crying immediately.

After you treated me, it was amazing: I could not even visualize the appointment! I still can't. My blood pressure returned to normal, and for the first time in a long time, I feel calm. When you told me my anxiety was now gone forever, I found it hard to believe, but so far so good!

Public Speaking

When perhaps a year ago you showed me how your havening procedure could cure fear of public speaking, the law of unexpected consequences manifested itself. I fearlessly began a late-life career as a public speaker, addressing audiences large and small on a myriad of subjects in varied venues.

But because of "remembrance of things past," I was afraid the efficacy of the treatment could fade in the middle of a speech, like the battery of my cell phone in the middle of a call, and I therefore utilize a reinforcement ritual. Immediately before rising to my feet to speak, I tap my left hand several times with my right, then the right with the left, tap the collarbone on both sides and then my forehead, roll my eyes to the ceiling, and recite the alphabet backwards and hum "Happy Birthday," in clear view of an astonished audience.

Generally, the reaction has been that I was suffering from St. Vitus dance, or performing a religious rite, similar to crossing oneself before attempting to kick a field goal, or having an allergic reaction to the awful food you get on the speaking circuit.

But obviously the treatment works, and, as an added benefit, the reinforcement ritual is the only physical exercise I get.

Fear of Snakes

Thank you for your help in dealing with my snake fears. Although I still do not understand how it works, I do know that it did. The recurring dream I've had twice a week since childhood, I have not had since you treated me. What a pleasure not to wake up two or three times each week anxiously checking under the bed and covers for snakes before being able to go back to sleep.

I also don't respond to photographs or snakes on TV shows or movies like I did in the past. This included running from a movie theater, leaving a child behind, when a snake appeared on the screen. It did not occur to me that I left a six-year-old in the theater until I reached the lobby.

When I used to see the image of a snake on TV I had to look under the chair, behind me, or under the covers or bed, depending on where

I was. As irrational as I know this was, I was not comfortable again until I made sure there was not a snake in the room. Now I don't have the same anxiety. I do turn away if I see a picture of a snake, but that's because it is ugly—I no longer feel the fear that I felt in the past. It is like it went from a 3D image to just a picture, and now is no longer threatening.

Grief Reduction

Since last Thursday's visit, when you performed that grief reduction procedure for me, I have continued to feel lighter and less sad when thinking about the death of my partner.

I noticed I have thought of him many more times during each day than I did prior to my visit with you—what I view as an interesting compensation for the lack of sadness intensity. Thank you for the "bearable lightness of being."

PTSD

I just had to let you know two things happened this weekend that [in the past] would have definitely caused an emotional reaction to what happened to my father that caused my PTSD—and nothing! I talked about it and I didn't get anxious or sad at all. I also heard a chainsaw, which was always a trigger for me because my father was cutting a tree with a chainsaw when I thought I saw him crushed to death.

Back Pain

Regarding the voodoo shaman juju stuff you did for my back, while I still have pain issues, the feedback loop of pain triggering stress triggering more pain, etc., is gone. One of the major benefits is that it allows me to focus clearly on the pain without fear, implementing remedial actions such as stretching or what little yoga I know, to help get it under control. Before, the panic response would prevent me from risking stretching out the muscles for fear something would "pop."

Back Pain

One week ago I came to your office in severe back pain. It was extremely difficult to bend or lean over, then try to stand erect. This could only be done by holding on to objects, i.e., chairs, tables, etc. I struggled with this more than a year, seeing physical therapists, taking medications, and even having a pain-killing device implanted in my back. After my visit, I can now bend, lean over, and stand straight up without holding on to anything, and more importantly, no pain. As you know, I also had a fear of public transportation, due to the major surgery I had one and a half years ago. Today I get on and off like everyone else and do not think about it twice.

Carrying a Chicken

My grandma Margaret always carried a chicken in her purse. It was broiled, then carefully wrapped in tinfoil so it wouldn't leak. I have a clear image of Gram's black purse with the gold clasp opening—on the playground, at the beach, in the shoe department at Best & Co. … and there was the chicken wrapped in foil. She also carried fruit, a few chocolate chip cookies, and little coffee-flavored sucking candies. I suppose she stored other things in there as well, like cash, keys, and makeup, but I never checked. I only remember the food.

My gram was 14 when her family emigrated from Hungary. I don't know who they left behind, or how terrible their living conditions became, or how many friends and relatives they eventually lost in the Holocaust.

My mom left Gram at 16 to become a dancer. She never returned or learned to cook. As an adult, I did my best to emulate Gram. By the time I was 40, I was a busy mom with three boys and a minivan filled with food. First, it was Cheerios in little baggies and juice boxes, then snacks like popcorn and peeled apples, maybe an occasional slice of pizza.

Years of being well prepared meant I never left the house without food in my car or my bag. Perhaps I didn't realize the food was also meant for me because it wasn't wrapped in foil. As the kids grew older, they only wanted money for the snack machines at school, but I noticed I still carried food with me. The groceries changed somewhat: For myself, I kept a supply of bran muffins for breakfast, power bars, peeled apples, cheese sticks, and Mentos for entertainment. I was ready for a long trip.

Eventually, of course, eating this car food was not without consequence and I needed help with my weight. I never left the house without food. When I discussed this with Dr. Ruden he said, "Let's try something." The treatment was gentle; he tapped and rubbed points on my face, had me hum a tune, count backwards, and move my eyes. Thoughts of anxiety, of leaving the house without food, seemed to diminish. The treatment sequence was repeated several times: I felt calmer about life in general, and definitely calmer about food.

I've actually started, yes, to leave the house without food. I have the clear sensation that I'll either be able to buy food wherever I go or be able to handle being hungry for a little while before I return home. I travel with a small purse now and lost those last tough 10 pounds!

Claustrophobia and Elevators

I felt a stirring in my stomach as I approached the elevator doors and couldn't differentiate between being frightened or just plain excited about testing the treatment you performed on me. Upon entering the elevator, the stirring ceased and, for a moment, I chatted with my husband, not even realizing I was on the dreaded elevator. I did, however, look up as we approached my floor and felt nothing! Not even a bit of discomfort. I almost felt as if something was missing from the ride (imagine!).

Rats

For years I had a terrible fear of rodents, to the point of experiencing horrific nightmares. I would wake up in a sweat, usually crying. One day my fear became a reality! I came home to find a little creature scurrying about. I went into immediate hysteria and ran out of my apartment. My anxiety was so severe I could not return home.

After two sessions with you, I was not only able to return home, but was quite proud of the fact that I was able to confront, literally, my worst nightmare! I have not had one dream since our work together.

Fear of Falling

I fell down a flight of "old Victorian stairs" with metal grippers and severed half my leg. Fortunately, I was able to keep my leg, but not without complications. In any case, since my accident, I find I am very sensitive to others' near accidents. An example of this is watching someone trip or me holding on to the railing very tight as I go downstairs, looking at each step. I didn't have much fear before my accident, but the reality set in and I have been having a hard time shaking it. Two weeks after your treatment, I was in a hurry to get somewhere and I was going down a flight of stairs. I noticed I was running down the stairs without holding on to the railing. I stopped halfway down, thought about the procedure you did on me and how you said at the end "you won't have any more anxiety about your accident." I laughed out loud and skipped, without holding on to the railing the rest of the way down. When I got to the bottom I jumped off as if I were a little kid. What a relief ... freedom!

Nasal Congestion

I asked if you could refer me to an ear, nose, and throat specialist for the chronic congestion in my left nostril. You questioned me about when it began. I told you it began after I hit my nose on a fence running out of the woods after being frightened. You had me recall the event and, applying gentle touch, had me do some humming and counting. After you were done, I couldn't believe it, seven years of congestion just disappeared!

Appendix A: Nontouch Havening*

On occasion, and with the permission of the client, I have had observers in the room, generally stationed behind the client and able to watch the therapy being performed. It has not escaped my notice that invariably, attentive observers felt calm after the treatment was over. They became relaxed after simply observing the therapy, without my ever having touched them. At first, this was puzzling, as I had postulated that the touch itself was critical to the outcome of havening. How could one be comforted and made to experience calmness and relaxation without being touched?

Mirror Neurons

The answer may lie in a group of neurons called mirror neurons. An Italian research group[1] seeking to explore the brain's response produced by visually observing an action by another was the first to describe mirror neurons. They were astonished to discover that both doing and observing an action activated similar neurons. Why should this be? These workers suggested that these mirror neurons played an important role in learning done through imitating actions,

---

* (see p. 14 in text)

for example, see then do. Indeed, many world-class athletes train by watching themselves performing a task. In addition, researchers studied clients both observing others experiencing emotions and feeling the same emotions themselves. Here, too, they discovered the same groups of neurons would fire under either circumstance. This, they felt, was the source of empathy, feeling what others feel when observing them. Language and other learning processes seemed also to use the mirror neuron system. Maldevelopment of the mirror neuron system is felt by some researchers to be the root cause of autism.

Functions mediated by mirror neurons depend on the anatomy and physiological properties of the circuit in which these neurons are located. Motor behavior was studied in the initial mirror neuron research. Accordingly, activations were found in circuits related to motor action. Later studies involving exposure to disgusting odorants and viewing movie clips showing individuals displaying a facial expression of disgust found that similar pathways were activated. Data have been obtained for sensory pain and seeing a painful situation experienced by another person loved by the observer.[2] Taken together, these experiments suggest that generating emotions by thought activates circuits that also mediate the corresponding emotion generated by extrinsic stimuli.[3] It should come as no surprise that watching someone being havened would have a response similar to that of the person actually being havened. The implication of this is of interest. One could theoretically make a movie of havening and use that to treat others merely by having them activate the problem while watching the video.

References

1. Rizzolatti, G., & Craighero, L. (2004). The mirror neuron system. *Annu. Rev. Neurosci.* 27:169–192.
2. Saarela, M. V., Hlushcuk, Y., Williams, A. C., Schurmann, M., Dalso, E., & Hari, R. (2007). The compassionate brain: Humans detect intensity of pain from another's face. *Cereb. Cortex* 17:230–237.
3. Gallese, V., Keysers, C., & Rizzolatti, G. (2004). A unifying view of the basis of social cognition. *Trends Cognitive Neurosci.* 8:396–403. Retrieved from http://www.scholarpedia.org/article/Mirror_neurons

Appendix B: Cultivating Resilience*

While some are traumatized by an event, others are not. As mentioned in the text, there are four requirements that need to be met for an event to be traumatizing. One of these components is the suitable landscape of the brain. First, we must define **psychological resilience**. In simplest terms, it is the capability of a landscape to resist being altered, or being able to rapidly return to a level that does not meet the requirements for traumatization. Resilience, therefore, increases the threshold to traumatization. How can this be accomplished?

Asking someone how they recovered from a trauma can do this. This provides an opportunity to learn how others have found solutions to stressful experiences. This learning process increases a belief in the ability to solve problems. By improving these skills, it enables us to cope better. Holding this belief, even if the problem is not solvable at the moment, reduces the risk of traumatization. These skills can include communication skills, problem-solving techniques, previewing (the ability to plan), and resource management. The goal of this process, what we wish to achieve, is a modulated response to an

* (see p. 50 in text)

intense emotional situation. Like any skill set, this requires practice. Amazingly, none of this is taught in schools. While certain inherent characteristics make individuals more or less susceptible, all can improve. This curriculum has been described and is outlined in a book by Dr. Tony Newman called *Promoting Resilience: A Review of Effective Strategies for Childcare Services*. This book in its entirety can be downloaded from www.ripfa.org.uk/aboutus/archive//files/reports. PromotingResilience.pdf.

Aside from formal teaching, nonspecific approaches such as yoga and meditation can be used. Techniques that decrease levels of stress hormones raise the threshold to traumatization. Staying fit is an excellent example, as it removes the stress of an out-of-shape body. Proper sleep, good food, loving attachments, and the practice of effort and reward, wherein effort toward an attainable goal is rewarded, are among these trainable approaches.

An unusual approach developed by primitive cultures involves the use of totems to aid the individual. Although not for everyone, the idea is to find a living object, be it animal or plant, that contains some of what is already part of you and has attributes that you wish to acquire. For example, you might find that the beauty of a hummingbird, along with its agility and skill, would fit you. Or a monkey who grooms its tribe members so that in turn it will be groomed, or the loyalty of penguins, or the rapid growth of a vine, or the power of a religious symbol, and so on. As part of healing, I have asked patients so inclined to choose a totem. One patient chose a blade of grass. When I asked why she chose this as her totem, she replied, "Because every time it gets mowed down it grows back." Ascribing special powers to these totems and extracting them for our own use can be of great use in enhancing resilience.

Carl C. Bell describes some characteristics of resiliency in his article "Cultivating Resiliency in Youth" (www.giftfromwithin.org/ html/cultivat.html). He describes the personality traits, abilities, characteristics, and spiritual approaches that increase resilience:

Have curiosity and intellectual mastery
Have compassion with detachment
Have the ability to conceptualize

Have the conviction of one's right to survive
Possess the ability to evoke images of good and sustaining figures
Be in touch with one's feelings
Have a goal
Have the ability to attract and use support
Have the need and ability to help others
Resourcefulness
Have a sense of true self
Develop "kokoro" (heart), a fighting spirit
Have a totem

William Osler, the founder of Johns Hopkins Medical School, in his address to the first graduating class, offered one way of developing resilience. Here, his totems are men. He writes:

> It is sad to think that, for some of you, there is in store disappointment, perhaps failure. You cannot hope, of course, to escape from the cares and anxieties incident to professional life. Stand up bravely, even against the worst. Your very hopes may have passed on out of sight, as did all that was near and dear to the Patriarch at the Jabbok ford, and, like him, you may be left to struggle in the night alone. Well for you, if you wrestle on, for in persistency lies victory, and with the morning may come the wished-for blessing. But not always; there is a struggle with defeat that some of you will have to bear, and it will be well for you in that day to have cultivated a cheerful equanimity. Remember, too, that sometimes "from our desolation only does the better life begin." Even with disaster ahead and ruin imminent, it is better to face them with a smile, and with the head erect, than to crouch at their approach. And, if the fight is for principle and justice, even when failure seems certain, where many have failed before, cling to your ideal, and, like Childe Roland before the dark tower, set the slug-horn to your lips, blow the challenge, and calmly await the conflict. (see www.medicalarchives.jhmi.edu/osler/aeqtable.htm for the complete essay.)

I read this on my first day of practice.

Appendix C: An Analysis of Fear of Flying*

Carrie experienced severe anxiety about flying. Days before a flight she would begin thinking about it and become very agitated. She avoided flying where possible and needed to take medicine before she could board a plane. She dates this to a particularly bad flight on a smallish plane where the turbulence was extreme. Since that time she feared flying, and after 9/11 it became even worse.

If you are afraid to fly, you may be suffering from aviaphobia.

A phobia is defined as a marked and persistent fear that is excessive or unreasonable, cued by the presence or anticipation of a specific object or situation. Thus, thought, like one of the five senses, can also activate the fear response merely by bringing the object or situation to mind. For someone with aviaphobia, the thought of being on a plane can produce fear.

This brief introduction to conquering the fear of flying will not provide statistics about safety, explain the funny sounds you hear when you are flying, or familiarize you with the aircraft. That would be a waste of time. Irrational fear does not lend itself to amelioration

---

* (see p. 70 in text)

by rational calculation. What we will do is to understand how the problem was encoded in your brain and how we can get rid of it.

What is fear? Fear is a survival response. It makes us ready to fight or run for our lives. It tenses our muscles, makes us breathe harder, and can make us aware of our heart. It causes us to sweat, we are uncomfortable, our thoughts race. "Let's get out of here!" our mind yells. Muscle tone increases, pupils dilate, and we focus on escape. This biological orchestration is meant to improve our chances of survival, literally causing us to feel our life is at stake.

Sitting in business class, cruising at 35,000 feet with a drink in our hand, hardly qualifies as a life-threatening situation. Yet many become terrified, but when they look around no one else seems scared. It is difficult to explain to someone who has not experienced it. In medical terms it's called phobic anxiety or, in the extreme, a panic attack. You may think you are going to die. You can try to explain to yourself that there is no danger, but your brain and body tell you differently. Your brain always wins.

Since fear is a response to a survival need, rapid action is required. No long analysis, no pondering options, just action. The emotion of fear is what makes us want to act. Here's how it works. Sensory input—the fact that you are on a plane, the fact there are some funny noises, the fact that there is some turbulence—is first sent to an area called the thalamus, sort of a central post office for incoming sensory information. This is the first stop before information is sent either to the amygdala directly or to the thinking and evaluation part of our brain called the cortex.

The amygdala was designed to make us better at survival by making us vigilant, preparing for flight or fighting and motivating us to action. Under normal conditions a fear response is generated by a stimulus that is evolutionarily hardwired to signal a threat. In order to maximize survival, the system needed to identify threats the first time. Sometimes you don't get a second chance. It needed to have hardwired patterns that shouted danger. There are fear stimuli that provoke action and vigilance in all animals. These are called **unconditioned fear stimuli** and they include:

A closed space
An open space

Loud noises
Low-pitched sounds (think *Jaws*)
Heights
Creepy-crawly slithery things
Things out of left field
Fear of injury or pain or being killed
Fear of suffocation
Things that feel slimy

If a pattern of an unconditioned fear stimuli (UFS) is recognized, it is sent to both the amygdala and the cortex of the brain. The pathway to the amygdala is almost instantaneous, while the cortex processing takes a little longer.

Sensory input (UFS pattern) → Thalamus → Amygdala → Fear Response

The signal from the cortex to the amygdala can either inhibit or sustain the response.

Thalamus → Cortex → Processed information → Pattern analyzed → ± Amygdala Activation

Under normal circumstances, when evaluation of these signals proves not to be of any danger, the prefrontal cortex (where we evaluate danger) sends an inhibitory signal to the amygdala and the fear response is stopped. This is a clever and simple solution. So while we might jump when walking in the woods and seeing something move in the grass, cortical evaluation shows it is just a stick (not a snake) and we calm down.

Medial prefrontal cortex → Amygdala → No fear

If there were never a plane crash or near miss or other mental image of this big bird falling out of the sky, you would think we would not have fear of flying. But we are in an aluminum tube 35,000 feet above the ground traveling at 300 mph with no way of getting off until the plane lands. There are plenty of reasons to be afraid to fly.

Let us look at all the unconditioned fears that arise from a plane ride:

1. Heights
2. Being trapped

3. Fear of being killed
4. Strange noises
5. Changes in altitude (turbulence causes a feeling in the stomach as if you were falling)
6. Fear of terrorists or a hijacking

You look out the window and the ground recedes from your view and you wonder how this multi-ton thing stays afloat on nothing but air. (The physics of airflow over a wing, giving it lift, is quite interesting but not of relevance here.) Height also comes into play in an unusual way, and it is involved with the experience of turbulence. During turbulence, the plane might suddenly drop and you have that funny feeling in the pit of your stomach. This feeling is an UFS as it occurs only when you are rapidly falling (it is unclear why this feeling occurs, but you immediately know its consequences, and you are afraid you will be killed). This fear might arise from childhood, when at one time you were frightened on a roller coaster. After reaching the top of the first hill, you were dropped precipitously, and both fear of heights and falling occurred at the same time the feeling in the stomach was happening. If traumatized at that moment, you then associate that feeling in the stomach with fear, so when there is turbulence and the plane dips, you experience the fear.

You are on a plane and the doors of the plane close: You are trapped. You hear a strange noise, or turbulence makes you feel that you are falling. You look out the window as the ground recedes. Now there is a big problem: There is no escape. Inescapability is the key. There is nowhere to run. If the landscape of the brain is appropriate, fear and traumatization occur.

Now every time you think of being on the plane, you are conditioned to have a fear response. We can now look at the plane as a conditioning stimulus. This fear can generalize and lead to a fear of going to the airport, of packing your suitcase, or of ordering your boarding pass days before the flight. You have been conditioned. You now have a fear of flying.

If everyone is exposed to these UFS, why doesn't everyone have a fear of flying? The answer is that they have not been traumatized.

Since being on a plane is inescapable, it is the meaning, the previous experiences, and the person's temperament that decide who becomes traumatized. If you have had relatives who died in a plane crash or have seen it happen, you are more susceptible. If you generally feel anxious, you are more susceptible to developing a phobia.

Extinguishing a Phobia

So how does one cure a phobia? There are several ways, including:

Havening, EMDR, and EFT
Cognitive therapy
Systematic desensitization

These approaches have success in treating a long-standing fear of flying. Havening begins by taking a good history. Asking about pre-disposing factors is helpful in determining the landscape of the brain. Many with a fear of flying can relate it to an event or specific flight. Others can acquire it from hearing about it from a parent or friend or watching a scary movie about a plane in trouble. Many anecdotal reports showed a marked increase in fear of flying after 9/11. The therapist should ask about related phobias, such as claustrophobia or height phobia, which need to be addressed as part of the treatment of the fear of flying. Indeed, there may be related issues, such as a pre-existing need to feel in control. These issues become important when havening is incomplete or unsuccessful.

In Practice

We have the client imagine the process of preparing to go to the airport, checking bags, going through security, handing in the ticket, sitting down (generally I have the client in a window seat in the back of the plane and an overweight individual sitting on the aisle), taking off, and landing. This activates most of the associated parts of the fear of flying. We then address other aspects that are troublesome as identified by the client, such as turbulence. At the end we teach self-havening and have the client practice and perform it if there is any activation of fear during this process.

The success rate is extremely high if a thorough evaluation is done.

Carrie was able to produce a fear response by bringing an upcoming plane flight into her imagination. Havening brought the subjective unit of distress (SUD) score from a 9 to a 3 but could not lower it further. Further history taking told of the flight where this began, and this was havened. Although a little better, the SUD score of getting on a plane could not be brought to 0. She then disclosed that it was the turbulence that was most frightening, and that she had a similar feeling on a roller coaster ride when she was little. Remarkably, she could bring that distant (over 50 years ago) memory back and it still produced a fear response! This was havened and brought the SUD score to 0. She has now been able to fly comfortably and on occasion will self-haven if she feels a little anxious.

Appendix D: Nightmares, Night Terrors, Just Bad Dreams, and Havening*

This essay is a theoretical and highly speculative analysis of the use of havening for recurrent dreams. While this essay focuses on nightmares and night terrors, any distressing dream can be treated, and with it the underlying issues. Dreams are suffused with confusing symbolism and metaphorical meaning. Why does the mind make dreams such a mystery? Freud believed the images presenting in dreams were disguised or manifest because during sleep, even though the barrier between the subconscious and conscious mind becomes more fluid, the frightening or offensive material would still need to be censored to avoid causing distress.

To uncover the true identity of the symbol, an analysis of the dream was required. During this process, elements of the dream (thoughts or feelings) could be used as clues for the client to free associate. Through the process of free association, the true latent (undisguised) meaning could be divined. The process is similar to archeology, like digging in ruins with many doors, seeking the door to the King's chamber.

---

* (see p. 91 in text)

How does the subconscious mind choose the symbols that arise during dreams? Freud felt that the symbols were acceptable alternatives to unacceptable thoughts and feelings.

Modern-day analysis of how information is stored in the brain-mind provides another view. Objects are stored in categories either as a prototype (where the object is the composite of many of the same type of an object, e.g., "dogness") or as a group of exemplars (exemplars are groups of objects that share much in common). How the mind-brain does this selection, though, remains unclear. Recurring dreams are of interest because they reflect not the content of the dream, but the affect. The feeling remains the same, but we have different story lines, with different characters. We dream of being chased, of standing naked, of being unprepared, of being trapped, and so on. All produce anxiety. While dream interpretation can vary, the specific reason for the dream often remains unknown to the dreamer. Some researchers suggest the purpose of a recurrent anxiety dream is to find an escape, a haven so that the ending is changed and repetition is avoided.

During dreaming, which occurs during rapid eye movement (REM) sleep and non-REM (NREM), changes in neuromodulator release occur. In REM sleep, both norepinephrine and serotonin levels dramatically drop. What are the consequences of the loss of these neurochemicals? The lack of norepinephrine, we speculate, diminishes the logical connectivity between narrative of the dream and the objects chosen for the dream. It means that the mind-brain goes to a location where the prototype/exemplars are stored and chooses one to be brought into the dream. Thus, in the category of male figures could be your best friend, grandfather, father, teacher, and so on.

The lack of serotonin decreases the threshold to association, broadening the categories from which symbols can be used. This only further hinders recognizing the origin of the symbol.

Night terrors are different. As David Richards points out (excerpted by permission from www.nightterrors.org):

> People who have night terrors are often misdiagnosed. The most common
> incorrect diagnosis is a simple nightmare. Any of you who have had a

night terror can say they aren't even close! Another common misdiagnosis (especially among veterans) is PTSD. For this reason I have included a description of the difference between nightmares and night terrors.

> **Night Terrors Symptoms:** Sudden awakening from sleep, persistent fear or terror that occurs at night, screaming, sweating, confusion, rapid heart rate, inability to explain what happened, usually no recall of "bad dreams" or nightmares, may have a vague sense of frightening images. Many people see spiders, snakes, animals or people in the room, are unable to fully awake, difficult to comfort, with no memory of the event on awakening the next day.

> **Night Terror or Nightmare:** Nightmares occur during the dream phase of sleep known as REM sleep [stage 2]. Most people enter the REM stage of sleep sometime after 90 minutes of sleep. The circumstances of the nightmare will frighten the sleeper, who usually will wake up with a vivid memory of a long movie-like dream. Night terrors, on the other hand, occur during a phase of deep non-REM sleep usually within an hour after the subject goes to bed.... During a night terror, which may last anywhere from five to twenty minutes, the person is still asleep, although the sleepers [*sic*] eyes may be open. When the subject does wake up, they usually have no recollection of the episode other than a sense of fear. This, however, is not always the case. Quite a few people interviewed can remember portions of the night terror, and some remember the whole thing.

Unlike nightmares, there is no escape from a night terror; awakening does not appear to be an option. Night terrors are probably the equivalent of a daytime panic attack for which no plan is available and the decision-making processes, usually entrusted to the prefrontal cortex, are taken off line. The lack of awakening suggests that the part of the brain that allows access to conscious awareness is blocked.

Nightmare Therapy

Nonetheless, if, as we speculate, the emotional state is the glue that ties together the components of a traumatization, and if a recurrent nightmare is the result of a traumatization, recalling the dream and generating an emotional response followed by havening should disrupt the path that activates the emotion.

Clinically, the client should bring the feeling state to conscious awareness by recalling the dream and generate a subjective unit of distress (SUD) score. This should activate the pathway through the BLC. There is no need to interpret or understand its symbolic meaning. If an event is recurrent, then this procedure should not only prevent the reoccurrence of the dream, but also remove the traumatization itself. If a client awakens after a recurrent nightmare, they should attempt self-havening the emotional distress until the SUD reaches zero.

Dr. Sergio Serrano suggests a simple routine to follow (http://www.emofree.com/Articles2/eft-dreams-core-issues.htm):

1. Before falling asleep, tell yourself that dreams are important and that you wish to remember them if you naturally awake.
2. If you awaken in the night, immediately replay the dream as vividly and as clearly as you can, focusing on the emotional content of the dream. Apply self-havening (Dr. Serrano applies tapping).
3. Return to sleep after the emotional response has been eliminated.
4. If you do not awaken during the night but can recall the dream during the day, apply havening after activation of the emotional content of the dream.

This technique can be used for any distressing dream or, for that matter, any distressing intrusive thought, such as those seen with PTSD. Further research is required to determine the efficacy of this approach.

Appendix E: Suggestions for Treatment*

An infinite number of different behaviors, physical ailments, and emotional states can be stored during a traumatization. For the six psychological problems described in the text we have had excellent results. When there is an obsessive comorbid disorder we find that havening is not as effective.

Get a good history of onset, surrounding events, and previous emotional events. Try to find the emotional origin of the symptom. For physical complaints, I ask clients if there is any unresolved anger or if they were ever in a motor vehicle accident or suffered any accident. Seek out traumatized rage or unresolved fear and its associated components. In cases of neck and back pain I seek unresolved anger. There are often several people at whom the anger may be directed. For example, in cases of unresolved anger toward an abusing parent, anger can be directed at the spouse for allowing it to persist or a significant other who dismisses your experience and feelings. Sometimes the symptoms are encoded with unexpressed rage.

Try to get the individual with panic disorder to activate the last time he or she experienced a panic attack and haven the fear of the physical feelings (such as rapid heartbeat, difficulty breathing). Ask

---

* (see p. 97 in text)

what about the physical feelings make him or her frightened. For physical ailments, especially chronic pain, ask if an organic disease has been ruled out. If it has not, suggest that the client returns after a workup has been completed.

A family history of substance abuse should alert you to underlying psychological problems, both inherent and as a consequence of living in a household where this occurs. The need for continued history taking if the problem does not resolve after havening the putative emotional event is seen in the story below.

I was asked to see a physician who had just experienced a debilitating stroke. The circumstances surrounding the stroke were terrifying to him. The stroke occurred on a night when he was sleeping in the on-call room. He was awakened by the event and realized that he was in trouble. He tried to rise, but his paralyzed left side prevented him from standing and he fell to the floor. He started screaming "Help me! I don't want to die here" over and over. After a while his shouts were heard and he was brought to the ER. Treatment began, but it was too late to reverse the damage. After a short stay in the hospital, he was moved to a rehabilitation facility. A week or so after arrival there, he would awaken about 90 minutes after falling asleep with the most excruciating pain, unresponsive to narcotic painkillers, in his paralyzed foot. By the time I had been asked to see him he had had this pain for several months.

Initially, the frightening memory of his lying on the floor screaming was havened. While he could no longer retrieve the cognitive or emotional components of that memory, his foot pain remained. On further detailed questioning about previous injuries he recalled an event 50 years prior when he was playing tennis and severely twisted that ankle, causing him to fall to the ground in pain. That position on the ground was similar to that which occurred during the stroke. I asked him to recreate the memory and he developed a subjective unit of distress (SUD) score of 7 (out of 10). After 50 years! This was havened and he slept through the next night without pain. He has remained pain-free since.

An interesting question arises as to why he developed pain many weeks after the original stroke. Ninety minutes after falling asleep corresponds to the first onset of REM sleep. Here both norepinephrine and serotonin levels drop dramatically and acetyl choline rises. One can postulate that during dreaming he subconsciously associated the earlier traumatized tennis accident due to overlap of the physical position on the ground. The traumatically encoded pain associated with that event, in the absence of norepinephrine, produced the severe pain. The lack of responsiveness to narcotics was because the pain did not arise from the periphery; rather, it was encoded centrally during the traumatization and did not involve an opioid-dependent pathway.

There are also times when the person has a great sense of shame or embarrassment about an event. Do no press this discussion, as it is not necessary for the therapist to understand the problem, only that the individual can bring the event and its emotional component to conscious awareness.

After getting a history that provides what you believe is the origin of the problem, have the client activate the emotional state.

Many aspects of a traumatized event and its sequelae need to be havened. One should haven the accident, fear of reinjury, fear of movement, fear of being permanently disabled, and other fears that the client relates. Modulate your voice in cadence and tone, and speak in an unhurried way. Self-havening can be useful for people with difficulties with being touched.

1. Learn from clues that reveal themselves as one disrupts the memory. Patients will often have an insight after a round of havening.
2. Consider using affirmations as well: "Even though I have this pain, this feeling, etc., I know I will be fine." (See Gary Craig's approach at www.eftuniverse.com)
3. Be persistent and aware. When clients get stuck and the SUD score cannot be lowered to 0, look elsewhere or earlier in the history for clues.
4. Abreactions in which the patient starts losing emotional control require the therapist to make a judgment whether to continue. These abreactions include crying, shaking, anger, fear, and other strong reactions to the imaginal event evoked by the client. I have found that using a firm voice and saying "Stay with me and focus on my what I need you to do," while simultaneously applying havening touch, can often disrupt these abreactions.

5. Use suggestions during the distracting part of havening; for example, as you walk up the flight of stairs, each step causes you to become calmer.

6. A traumatization should cause you to seek out previous traumatizing episodes. In this way we might prevent future events from being traumatizing. Indeed, searching for earlier clues may require going back to the earliest parts of our young life, when our memories are not readily available because the part of the brain that stores narrative has not developed. Asking the client to ask his or her parents may provide important clues. While this is not easy, we must actively seek out these feelings because, although hidden, they affect how we respond to the present moment.

In the final analysis, if we disrupt the linkage between the emotion and the cognitive component of the event, the other components also lose their ability to be reactivated. I think that it is useful to consider havening as providing a sense of safety that allows us to de-traumatize the event. For an excellent book on futher ideas and approaches, see Wells, S., & Lake, D. (2010) *Enjoy Emotional Freedom*. Wollambi, Australia: Exisle Publishing Limited.

Appendix F: Transduction, Depotentiation, and the Electrochemical Brain*

The model presented in this book is an electrochemical one. The key chemical players are those neurochemicals that "landscape" the brain and are associated with vigilance, salience, and a feeling of safety. Touch stimuli (as well as other sensory stimuli) enter the brain and are transduced (converted) into both electrical and chemical signals. The duality of this signal is similar to the particle-wave nature of light. What we measure is what we observe.

Thus, when we study the electrical brain with an electroencephalogram (EEG), we are measuring the electrical components of firing neurons. These electrical components are measured as waves. EEGs can be modified by the use of chemicals injected into the brain. We can use specific chemical substances such as GABA agonists (an agonist acts as if it were the substance itself) to alter the EEG. GABA agonists and acetyl choline (a neurochemical also involved with learning) have been shown to increase a specific waveform associated with 1 to 2 Hz called a delta wave.

---

* (see p. 107 in text)

Suffice it to say that there is no electrical activity without neuro-chemicals and no neurochemical release without electrical activity.

Rasolkhani-Kalhorn and Harper[1] speculate that synapses mediat-ing traumatic memories found in the BLC have a larger than usual number of specific glutamate receptors. They are in agreement with other research showing that exposure therapies open these glutamate receptors, thus making these memory traces labile and subject to dis-ruption. Memories, they suggest, are extinguished by the depotentia-tion and elimination of these glutamate receptors by a 1-to 2-Hz signal generated directly as a result of touch, tapping, and eye movement. They provide evidence from EEG studies of subjects undergoing eye movement desensitization and reprocessing (EMDR) that eye move-ments or tapping (nonspecific brain stimulation) enhances a preexist-ing 1.5-Hz neuronal firing frequency of principal neurons in the areas of activated pathways.

According to Harper and colleagues,[2] traumatic memory is reac-tivated by an overpotentiated glutamate receptor called alpha-amino-3-hydroxy-5-methyl-4-isoxazolproprioninc (AMPA). We suggest that EMDR, EFT, TFT-CT, and havening increase the amplitude of a depotentiating wave by raising GABA. Depotentiation occurs through the internalization of the activated glutamate receptors. This permanently removes activated AMPA receptors, preventing the neu-ron from propagating the traumatic memory and its components.

This electrical model has simplicity and experimental evidence to provide us with a good idea as to how havening disrupts the trau-matic memory. The chemical model helps us understand how we feel after havening.

References

1. Rasolkhani-Kalhorn, T., & Harper, M. L. (2006). EMDR and low fre-quency stimulation of the brain. *Traumatology* 12:9–24.
2. Harper, M. L., Rasolkhani-Kalhorn, T., & Drozd, J. F. (2009). On the neu-ral basis of EMDR therapy: Insights from qEEG studies. *Traumatology* 15:81–95.

Appendix G: Havening Touch: Clinical Guidelines*

Even though touch is used in many therapeutic situations, its use in the practice of psychotherapy has been essentially forbidden. While nail salon workers, massage therapists, physical therapists, dentists, and doctors touch their clients, trained talk therapists do not.

Freud set the stage for our current-day situation by describing touch between the therapist and client as having the potential for erotic misinterpretation. As a consequence, the practice of psychoanalysis and other talk psychotherapies became touch averse. In the setting of havening therapy I have found that a simple explanation that the purpose of havening touch is to provide a sense of safety removes the act from the sexual arena and places it in a therapeutic context. During the last six years, I have never had havening touch experienced in any way other than therapeutic.

Touch is arguably the most powerful form of communication. The extrasensory response to touch can alleviate pain, produce a sense of belonging, and provide for feelings of acceptance and trust. Touch is particularly important for the elderly, who are often untouched and lonely. Most of us are probably touch deprived.

_____

* (see p. 115 in text)

What areas of the body produce a sense of safety? We believe, and as has been shown by Field[1], it is the areas that come in regular contact with the parent. These areas are the face and head, the arms and hands. The simple act of holding hands has powerful extrasensory effects.

While the research has yet to be done, common sense suggests that the extrasensory components of touch are more powerful when applied by another. Tickling is an example. Nonetheless, self-touching is powerful in and of itself. A client can self-haven with the image of someone who the client wishes to perform the havening in mind. From the theoretical model described in this book,

I was teaching a woman who had several phobias and chronic fatigue how to self-haven. I told her to cross her arms and gently rub the upper arm on the other side. She suddenly stopped, gasped, and started to release tears. She said that she just recalled and experienced how wonderful and comforting it was when her father did that to her.

If havening is applied outside the psychotherapeutic setting, such as an internist's practice, no problems should arise. However, if it is used as part of a psychotherapeutic treatment, careful deliberation should precede its use. This may be a moot problem, however, because if a therapist feels uncertain in any way, self-havening touch can be taught to the client and self-applied.

Durana provides six guidelines to help the therapist when it is determined that touch is appropriate:[2]

1. The therapist must learn about the client's readiness for touch.
2. Before touching, the therapist must determine the appropriateness of potential contact and advise the client as to areas of touch.
3. The therapist must be aware of how the client interprets the contact.
4. The therapist must be aware of his or her own feelings.
5. The client's family may misconstrue physical contact, and education of the family may be necessary.
6. Decision to touch should be based solely on the client's needs.

When used in this manner, havening touch, distraction, and other mild brain stimulation are powerful agents for change. It is sad that the mental health profession ignores such powerful tools, as they often lead to a deeper understanding of the client's problems and resolve issues that are not accessible simply by talk therapy.

References

1. Field, T., Diego, M. & Hernandez-Reif, M. (2005). Massage therapy research. *Dev. Rev.* 27: 75–89.
2. Durana, C. (1998). The use of touch in psychotherapy: Ethical and clinical guidelines. *Psychotherapy* 35:269–280. For more information, see www.zurinstitute.com/touchintherapy.html#guidelines and www.zurinstitute.com/touchstandardofcare.pdf

Appendix H: The Downside of Removing a Traumatic Memory*

Removing a distressful memory would seem to have only benefits, but there are circumstances when this is not the case. Attachment is strong in a traumatized memory, and the emotion it arouses keeps our connections alive. This is particularly true when you have lost a loved one. People are motivated by emotions, and a traumatizing event can be the driving force for someone's life work. Before treatment it is wise to ask the client whether he or she wishes to have the emotional component of the memory erased, and possibly the ability to visualize it altogether. It is important that we respect others' feelings, and not try to always make life less painful. Be aware that you will be changing how the individual perceives the world. For the most part, this is a good thing.

There is a medical joke that goes as follows: Sadie, who is 85 years old, calls her friend and screams to her, "I'm dead! I'm dead!" Her friend, alarmed by the statement, asks, "How do you know?" Sadie answers, "Nothing hurts."

---

* (see p. 118 in text)

Appendix I: Notes and Additional References

This section provides an annotated review of selected articles and books useful for understanding traumatization and havening therapy.

Chapter 1: A Third Pillar

Chapter 1 introduces the reader to traumatization and this will be called **havening**. Among the crucial issues facing modern medicine is that most health care providers do not recognize traumatization as a cause of symptoms. A few researchers and clinicians have attempted to bring this to the attention of mainstream medicine.

Tallis, F. (2002). *Hidden minds. A history of the unconscious.* New York, NY: Arcade Publishing.
This beautifully written book explores how the unconscious can affect our lives. Tallis describes the ideas and efforts of the early researchers, Charcot, Janet, Freud, Breuer, Jung, and other great scientists and thinkers, as they explore the unconscious. He comments on the intellectual searches, jealousies, battles, and disappointments these brilliant men experienced as they undertook to find passages into the hidden mind. Hidden minds will alter the way you think about the unconscious. See also Tallis's book *Changing Minds*.

Kirmayer, L. J., Lemelson, R., & Barad, M. (Eds.). (2007). *Understanding trauma. Integrating biological, clinical and cultural perspectives.* New York, NY: Cambridge University Press.

This book reviews the neurobiology of fear conditioning and extinction as well as the effects of early-life stress on the development of neural systems as they relate to vulnerability for traumatization. It describes the clinical consequences and current treatments for those who struggle with traumatization. This book also examines how massive traumatic events come to affect the whole of a society. In this regard, it goes beyond the simple laboratory or clinical descriptions and places traumatization as an engine of societal transformation. I particularly appreciated Rousseau and Meashm's chapter on posttraumatic suffering as a source of transformation.

Van der Kolk, B. A., McFarlane, A. C., & Weisaeth, L. (Eds.). (2007). *Traumatic stress. The effects of overwhelming experience on mind, body and society.* New York, NY: Guilford Press.

As we journey toward understanding trauma, this book is a must-read. It concerns the prototype of traumatic disorders: posttraumatic stress disorder (PTSD). Bessel A. van der Kolk and his coeditors have collated the knowledge that has accreted through decades of clinical, epidemiological, and neuroscience studies. These authors present new and exciting ideas about the disorder and its impact on the individual, society, and the world. The book discusses potential neurobiological mechanisms and uses these ideas to formulate treatment. This book is the paperback volume of the first edition, published in 1996, and its observations and constructs continue to guide research today. It is easy to become swept away by the sheer magnitude of its scope. Slow, thorough reading and rereading are necessary for an appreciation of what has been accomplished here.

Sarno, J. E. (2006). *The divided mind: The epidemic of mindbody disorders.* New York, NY: ReganBooks, HarperCollins.

John Sarno states (p. 1):

"Health care in America is in a state of crisis. Certain segments of American medicine have been transformed into a dysfunctional nightmare of irresponsible practices, dangerous procedures, bureaucratic regulations, and skyrocketing costs. Instead of healing people, the broken health care system is prolonging people's suffering in too many cases. Instead of preventing epidemics, it is generating them.

The enormity of this miscarriage of medical practice may be compared to what would exist if medicine refused to acknowledge the existence of bacteria and viruses. Perhaps the most heinous manifestation of this scientific medievalism has been the elimination of the term *psychosomatic* from the *Diagnostic and Statistical Manual of Mental Disorders* (DSM), the official publication of the American Psychiatric Association. One might as well eliminate the word *infection* from medical dictionaries."

While this may seem harsh, Dr. Sarno goes on to show how we have missed what is hidden in plain sight—how the mind and the body are connected. He uses decades of research to explore the origin and treatment of chronic pain, especially back pain, which afflicts millions of people. Every health professional should read this and come to his or her own conclusions.

Scaer, R. C. (2007). *The body bears the burden. Trauma, dissociation and disease.* Binghamton, NY: Haworth Press.
  This breakthrough book, following in the footsteps of Peter Levine (see p. xix in Scaer's book), is a challenging read, but the effort is worthwhile. Its fundamental premise is that a painful physical event that occurs during a traumatization is coencoded during the traumatizing event. The pain may or may not be experienced at the time of the event, but it is none-theless stored and experienced later. He describes the encoding moment as that of a freeze state, one of tonic immobility. Unless this freeze state is discharged, that is, motoric action taken, the mind keeps the fight-or-flight energy internally. It is this undischarged energy that causes the symptoms due to a traumatization. By releasing this energy, the event can be processed, the trauma erased, and the pain eliminated. Scaer brilliantly illuminates the origin of the puzzling picture of somatic problems that arise after a traumatic event.

Gay, P. (1989). *The Freud reader.* New York, NY: W.W. Norton & Co.
  The Western world is infused with Freudian ideas. His most original idea is the supremacy of the unconscious (which in this book we call the sub-conscious). We are told that the unconscious reveals itself in many ways, by slips of the tongue, by behavior, and by dreams. If we can enter that world and bring the unconscious to awareness, we may be able to affect a cure. Talking was the method Freud and others have used. Some of Freud's views remain with us today, while others have fallen out of favor, but his overall body of ideas remains a most impressive exploration of the human mind.

There are probably hundreds of systems of talk therapy. They are based on a variety of models for understanding the unconscious and how language interacts with the brain. These systems can be accessed and reviewed via Wikipedia.

Wikipedia has an excellent, brief discussion of **psychotherapy**, the first pillar (http://en.wikipedia.org/wiki/Psychotherapy).

In addition, Freud's work is essential to understanding a central theme in this book, the role of the unconscious. We have chosen to use the word *subconscious* instead of *unconscious* so that it includes memories both inaccessible and accessible by conscious thought.

Wikipedia also has an excellent brief discussion of **psychopharmacology,** the second pillar (http://en.wikipedia.org/wiki/ Psychopharmacology). Discussions of individual medications and where they work in the brain can be found in the many psychopharmacology texts available from online booksellers or medical libraries.

Chapter 2: The Role Emotions Play

Understanding emotions and the role they play in our lives allows us to appreciate their power and their necessity.

Canon, W. B. (1929). *Bodily changes in pain, hunger, fear and rage.* New York, NY: Harper Torchbooks.

> This is *the* classic book on the physiology of emotions. As Canon describes in his preface, "Fear, rage and pain, and the pangs of hunger are all primitive experiences which human beings share with lower animals." Canon then proceeds to illuminate how one maintains the integrity of the body. The concept of homeostasis (*homeo*, "same"; *stasis*, "state"), which means "keeping our insides stable," is introduced here. He discusses how our bodies keep us at 98.6 °F, regulate our blood sugar, and maintain our blood pressure whether standing, lying, or sitting. Canon describes what happens in our bodies when homeostasis is disturbed and how it reacts to counter these changes. He was the first to describe the effects of fear and hunger on physiological functions and the role of epinephrine. This book, published just under 100 years ago, is full of insights that help explain what we witness every day. It is a book of great medical historical importance, and while it is worthwhile to read, just skimming through the book connects you to the earliest work on stress.

Selye, H. (1978). *The stress of life.* New York, NY: McGraw-Hill.

> This book introduces the term *stress* to the biological vocabulary. Although some of his ideas are outdated, Selye's book is a thrill to read. Selye takes you through his early research, where he tries to understand why different stressors produced the same response. He was way ahead of his time in describing the role of stress on the immune, cardiovascular, gastrointestinal, musculoskeletal, neurological, and psychiatric systems. This book lays the foundation for mind-brain-body medicine and should be read by everyone interested in psychology.

Fellous, J.-M., & Arbib, M. A. Eds. (2005). *Who needs emotions? The brain meets the robot.* New York, NY: Oxford University Press.

This remarkable compilation of essays is directed toward trying to understand if robots could be constructed to think and experience emotions. An important idea discussed here is that emotions play many roles in survival. Their primary role is as an amplifier; that is, they increase the importance of an event to an individual and are fundamentally protective and useful for survival. Emotions also have many other secondary roles that are critical.

This book summarizes much of the literature on the organization and basic principles of emotion-producing systems and includes perspectives from a social interaction viewpoint.

The response to fear as described by Fellous and LeDoux in their chapter on emotional processing (p. 87) includes:

$$\text{Fear} \rightarrow \begin{array}{l} \text{Defensive behavior} \\ \text{Increased arousal} \\ \text{Increased pain threshold} \\ \text{Release of stress hormones} \\ \text{Decreased reflex time} \end{array}$$

These responses are all directed by the amygdala.

Reactive, routine, and reflective emotions are discussed in "Who Needs Emotions," by Ortony, Norman, and Revelle, on p. 179. Ralph Adolphs, in his chapter (pp. 9–28) "Could a Robot Have Emotions?" describes the various roles emotions provide for survival purposes. Some ideas are included in the main body of the text. A discussion of emotions as part of the motivational system is described by Ann E. Kelly. In her chapter (pp. 29–79) she describes the neurochemical networks encoding motivation. Here, both positive and negative emotions are part of this system. This book is remarkably readable and provides an introduction to emotions and their function.

Gazzaniga, M. S., Ivry, R. B., & Mangun, G. R. (2002). *Cognitive neuroscience: The biology of the mind.* New York, NY: W.W. Norton & Co.

This book introduces one to the field of cognitive neuroscience. Starting from the molecular, cellular, and anatomical aspects, it offers a wonderful overview of perception, encoding, learning, memory, emotion, and other topics considered to be amenable to scientific study. Cognitive neuroscience explores emotion by studying mind-brain interactions with psychophysical and brain imaging techniques such as fMRI, MRI, PET, and ERPs (event-related potentials). In essence, it reveals what parts of the brain are active when emotions are involved.

Lieberman, M. D., & Eisenberger, N. I. (2009). The pains and pleasures of social life. *Science* 323:890–891.

These scientists describe the neurobiological relationship between physical pains (hunger, thirst) and psychological pains (social exclusion, bereavement, unfairness, negative social comparison). These researchers argue that physical and psychological pain share common brain pathways.

Ruden, R. A., & Byalick, M. (2003). *The craving brain*. New York, NY: HarperCollins.

This book outlines in detail the consequences of chronic inescapable stress and its effect on the appetitive drive system. It speculates that chronic stress decreases serotonergic activity of the brain. This low level of serotonin sensitizes the nucleus accumbens so that it reacts compulsively to nonappetitive stimuli. Since these nonappetitive stimuli (e.g., cigarettes, alcohol) do not have a mechanism to shut down their consumption, addictive behavior results. Traumatization produces chronic inescapable stress and can set the stage for addictive behavior.

Chapter 3: Ancient Emotions and Survival

Fear and rage have been studied in animals, including humans. Some sources are listed below.

McFarland, D. (1987). *The Oxford companion to animal behavior*. New York, NY: Oxford University Press.

A clear understanding of how and why animals behave is available in this storehouse of information, readily accessible to the general public. Written by an international team of experts, it contains over 200 entries that range from aggression to courtship to facial expressions, flight, navigation, mate selection, and fear.

How fear and physiological changes are produced by sensory input is described in this book. This book describes fear as "a state of motivation that is aroused by certain stimuli and normally gives rise to defensive or escape behavior." In humans, fear has a unique facial expression that involves the platysma muscle and wide-open eyes. A dog's response to a threat is described here (p. 6):

When we look at the dog's external appearance in the threatening and defensive postures, they appear to be completely opposite. The threatened dog tries to make itself as large as possible. The self-defense posture is to protect vital parts. In humans, defensive rage is not aggression but it is the equivalent of the threatening posture. As a last resort we are trying to scare our adversary and want to look as ferocious as possible.

Each sense organ has a pathway to the amygdala that engages a fear response, and these are described in this book.

FIG. 20.—Terror, from a photograph by Dr. Duchenne.

Figure I.1 Charles Darwin showed this picture to 23 people, who were then asked to describe the emotional state of the person. (From Darwin, C., *Expression of the Emotions in Man and Animals*, D. Appleton & Co., New York, NY, 1898, p. 294.)

Darwin, C. (1898). *Expression of the emotions in man and animals.* New York, NY: D. Appleton & Co.

Darwin showed the picture seen in Figure I.1 (p. 294 of his book) to 23 persons who were asked to describe the emotional state of the person. Thirteen said horror, great pain; three answered extreme fright; six said anger; and one said disgust. All these feelings are closely related to a mental state of fear. This book is also among the classics that relate the similarity of human and nonhuman expressions of emotions and how all of us recognize them.

De Becker, G. (1997). *The gift of fear. Survival signals that protect us from violence.* New York, NY: Little, Brown, & Co.

True fear, De Becker states, is a gift. It is a survival signal that sounds only in the presence of danger. Through story and theory he describes how the subconscious alerts us and why we better pay attention.

LeDoux, J. (1996). *The emotional brain*. New York, NY: Touchstone Press.

This book, already a classic, brings together research on the physiology of emotions and their role in learning. LeDoux describes an experiment conducted by a French physician named Edouard Claparede in the early part of the last century. His patient seemingly lost her ability to make new memories, and each time they met he had to reintroduce himself. On one occasion he placed a pin in his hand such that when they shook hands, the patient received a painful prick. On the next visit, the patient refused to shake hands with him. She couldn't say why, but obviously the good doctor now came to represent pain and she was afraid.

LeDoux feels that this form of learning does not depend on conscious awareness, and once the learning takes place, the stimulus does not have to be consciously perceived to elicit the emotional response. This experiment sets the theoretical background for subconscious stimuli activating the amygdala.

In another part of the book LeDoux (pps. 258–261) describes the descent into panic: "As the amygdala is becoming increasingly active, it makes sense that the thinking portion be diminished and preprogrammed responses to danger take over so that decisions are not delayed because of an evaluation of the available options. This is not a conscious process; it is what Nature did to improve the chances of survival."

This was a groundbreaking book when published in 1996. It contains speculations, some which have been modified, but that is why ongoing research is so important (mostly done by LeDoux and coworkers), and theoretical models are made based on the best available evidence.

Shaikh, M. B., & Siegel, A. (1994). Neuroanatomical and neurochemical mechanisms underlying amygdaloid control of defensive rage behavior in the cat. *Braz. J. Med. Bio. Res.* 27:2759–2779.

It is well established that the hypothalamus and the periaqueductal gray (PAG) play important roles in the expression of defensive rage behavior. While defensive rage is not elicited from the amygdala, this region of the limbic system nevertheless serves an important role in the modulation of defensive rage behavior. The experimental data establish that activation of the basomedial region facilitates defensive rage. Activation of the central nucleus suppresses defensive rage. The suppression of defensive rage by the Ce makes sense because that area is used to engage the fight-or-flight mechanism.

Chapter 4: Memory and Emotion

We remember what arouses us. Without emotion our important memories would be difficult to retrieve.

Harley, C. W. (2004). Norepinephrine and dopamine as learning signals. *Neural Plast.* 11:191–204.

This article reviews the evidence that norepinephrine and dopamine act as learning signals. Both norepinephrine and dopamine are broadly distributed in areas concerned with the representation of the world and with the conjunction of sensory inputs and motor outputs. Both are released at times of novelty, uncertainty, and the emotions of fear and rage, providing a plausible signal for updating representations and associations. These substances activate intracellular machinery postulated to serve in the memory formation cascade.

Phelps, E. A. (2004). Human emotion and memory: Interactions of the amygdala and the hippocampus. *Curr. Opin. Neurobiol.* 14:198–204.

The amygdala and hippocampal complex are two structures deep within the medial temporal cortex. In emotional situations, these two systems are linked to each other in subtle but important ways. Specifically, the amygdala can modulate the encoding, storage, and retrieval of hippocampus-dependent memories. The hippocampus, by forming long-term representations of events of emotional significance, can influence the right amygdala's response when emotional stimuli are encountered. These systems act in concert when emotion meets memory.

Cahill, L. (1997). The neurobiology of emotionally influenced memory. Implications for understanding traumatic memory. *Ann. N.Y. Acad. Sci.* 821:238–246.

Substantial evidence from animal and human subject studies converges on the view that memory for emotionally arousing events is modulated by a memory system consisting, at a minimum, of stress hormones, the hippocampus, the amygdala, and the medial prefrontal cortex. Within the normal range of emotions experienced, this system is viewed as an evolutionary adaptive method of creating memory strength that is, in general, proportional to memory importance. In conditions of extreme emotional stress, the dysfunction of this normally adaptive system may underlie the formation of strong, intrusive memories characteristic of PTSD.

McGaugh, J. L. (2004). The amygdala modulates the consolidation of memories of emotionally arousing experience. *Annu. Rev. Neurosci.* 27:1–28.

Converging findings of animal and human studies provide compelling evidence that the amygdala is critically involved in enabling us to acquire and retain lasting memories of emotional experiences. Considerable data from animal studies indicate that (1) the amygdala mediates the memory-modulating effects of stress hormones; (2) the effects are selectively mediated by the basolateral complex of the amygdala (BLC); (3) the BLC modulates memory encoding via efferents to other brain regions, including the caudate nucleus, nucleus accumbens, and cortex; and (4) the BLC modulates the encoding of many different kinds of information. The findings of human brain imaging studies are consistent with those of animal studies, suggesting that activation of the amygdala influences the encoding of long-term emotional memory; the degree of activation of the amygdala by emotional arousal during encoding correlates with ease of subsequent recall. The activation of neuromodulatory systems affecting the BLC and its projections to other brain regions involved in processing different kinds of information plays a key role in enabling emotionally significant experiences to be well remembered.

Anderson, A. K. (2005). Affective influences on the attentional dynamics supporting awareness. *J. Exp. Psychol. Gen.* 134:258–281.

Emotionally arousing stimuli enhance long-term memory of immediately preceding neutral stimuli. The findings fit with the preservation-consolidation hypothesis. This hypothesis states that emotional arousal activates neurobiological processes that modulate the consolidation of memories of recent experiences. This arousal-induced modulation of memory is mediated by norepinephrine activation of the amygdala.

McIntyre, C. K., Power, A. E., Roosendaal, B., & McGaugh, J. L. (2003). Role of basolateral amygdala in memory consolidation. *Ann. N.Y. Acad. Sci.* 985:273–293.

Memories of emotionally arousing events tend to be more vivid and to persist longer than do memories of neutral or trivial events. Moreover, memories of emotionally influenced information may endure after a single experience. Recent findings strongly suggest that the influence of emotional arousal on memory consolidation is meditated by the release of adrenal stress hormones (epinephrine and cortisol) and neurotransmitters that converge on modulating the noradrenergic system within the amygdala. Considerable evidence also indicates that amygdala activation influences memory by regulating consolidation in other brain regions. This work supports the notion that the BLC acts as glue for the components of a traumatic memory.

Morenson, G. J., Jones, D. L., & Yim, C. Y. (1980). From motivation to action: Functional interface between the limbic system and the motor system. *Progr. Neurobiol.* 14:67–97.

This article describes the relationship between emotion and motion. It connects the limbic system with the nucleus accumbens and other downstream neural components that organize behavior and activate motivational states.

Ordway, G. A., Schwartz, M. A., & Frazer, A. (Eds.). (2007). *Brain norepinephrine.* Cambridge, UK: Cambridge University Press.

This book is intended for researchers and graduate students. Benno Roozendaal, PhD, writes a chapter on norepinephrine and long-term memory. Gary S. Aston-Johns writes a chapter on the locus coeruleus and regulation of behavioral flexibility and attention. Petrovaara Antti discusses norepinephrine and pain. There are many other excellent chapters. For those readers with a background in neuroscience, the chapters in this book provide a strong argument for norepinephrine as one of the key neurochemicals in encoding a traumatization.

Chapter 5: Encoding a Traumatic Memory

A single event can change your life. How does the brain make this happen?

Ferreira, T. L., Shammah-Lagnado, S. J., Bueno, O. F., Moreira, K. M., Fornari, & Oliviera, M. G. (2008). The indirect amygdala-striatum pathway mediates conditioned freezing: insights on emotional memory networks. Neuroscience 153(1) 84–94.

Where are emotional events stored prior to the hippocampus being operational? The dorsal striatum (made up of caudate and putamen nuclei) is involved with emotional learning. In a previous study (Ferreira, T. L., Moreira, K. M., Ikeda, D. C., Bueno, O. F. A. & Oliviera, M. G. M. (2003). Effects of dorsal striatum lesions in tone fear conditioning and contextual fear conditioning. *Brain Res.* 987:17–24), disruption of both right and left dorsal striatum was shown to disrupt fear tone conditioning. This study demonstrates that lesioning both the Ce of the amygdala and the dorsal striatum on the other side of the brain also impaired the acquisition of tone fear conditioning. This suggests that the striatum may be the location of fear memories in the absence of a functional hippocampus. It also suggests that if the dorsal striatum is intact an event may be accessible via a felt sense and thus be useful for activating the BLC to allow for havening.

Tully, K. Li, Y. Tsvetkov, E. & Bolshakov, V. Y. (2007). Norepinephrine enables the induction of associative long-term potentiation at thalamo-amygdala synapses. *Proceed. Nat. Acad. Sci.* 104(35):14146–14150.

This article argues for the role of norepinephrine in the production of long-term potentiation in the lateral nucleus of the amygdala. Information arriving from the thalamus under the influence of norepinephrine overrides GABA inhibition of the neurons leaving the lateral nucleus. This allows for pathways to be generated.

Chapter 6: Causes and Consequences of Traumatization

Saigh, P. A. (1991). The development of post-traumatic stress disorder following four different types of traumatization. *Behav. Res. Ther.* 29:213–216.

The Children's Post-Traumatic Stress Disorder Inventory was used to identify 230 cases of childhood PTSD. Of these cases, 58 had been traumatized through direct experience, 128 through observation, 13 through verbal mediation, and 31 by combinations thereof.

Van der Kolk, B. A., & Fisler, R. (1995). *Dissociation and the fragmentary nature of traumatic memories: Overview and exploratory studies.* Retrieved from http://www.trauma-pages.com/vanderk2.htm

The nature and reliability of traumatic memories and their role in the development of PTSD are controversial issues in psychiatry. This paper reviews studies collected from people's memories of highly stressful and traumatic experiences. It confirms Janet's clear distinction between a traumatic and an ordinary memory. According to Janet, a traumatic memory consists of images, sensations, and affective and behavioral states that are invariable and do not change over time. In contrast, ordinary memories are semantic and symbolic. These memories are social and adapted to the needs of both the narrator and the listener, and can be expanded, contracted, embellished, or diminished according to social demands. While a traumatic memory may leave indelible sensory and affective imprints, once these are able to become incorporated into a complete personal narrative as a nontraumatic memory (the traumatization is cured), it is subject to degrees of distortion similar to ordinary memory.

Ortiz, J. P., Close, L. N., Heinricher, M. M., & Selden, N. R. (2008). Alpha (2)-noradrenergic antagonist administration into the central nucleus of the amygdala blocks stress-induced hypoalgesia in awake behaving rats. *Neuroscience* 157:223–228.

Researches here tested the hypothesis that stress-induced release of norepinephrine into the central nucleus of the amygdala (Ce) mediates analgesia. Injection of clonidine, which mimics norepinephrine, into the central nucleus of the rat produced a dose-dependent increase in pain relief, compared to saltwater control in the tail flick latency test. This test measures how long it takes the rat to move its tail when it is subject to a painful stimulus; the longer it takes to move the tail, the greater the latency and the greater the analgesia. The analgesic effect was blocked by injection of the norepinephrine antagonist idazoxan. Injection of these substances elsewhere in the amygdala, including the BLC, had no effect.

Otis, J. D., Keane, T. M., & Kerns, R. D. (2003). An examination of the relationship between chronic pain and post-traumatic stress disorder. *J. Rehab. Res. Dev.* 40:397–406.

A substantial literature currently exists documenting the relationship between chronic pain and substance abuse, depression, and anxiety disorders. Several models are proposed and are of interest; however, none have been developed fully or tested.

Ruden, R. A. (2008). Encoding states: A model for the origin and treatment of complex psychogenic pain. *Traumatology* 14:119–126.

This article brings together the ideas of Scaer and Sarno. Here, pain coencoded with traumatized defensive rage and fear is the cause of complex psychogenic pain. This provides an opportunity to cure the painful conditions by havening the traumatic encoding moment.

Karen, R. (1998). *Becoming attached: First relationships and how they shape our capacity to love.* New York, NY: Oxford University Press.

Attachment provides meaning to an experience. Being detached from an experience prevents the expression of emotion and traumatization. How does attachment occur and what can go wrong? Karen's book is essential to understanding this process.

Karen takes us on a psychohistorical journey from the beginnings of attachment theory to its current incarnation. He discusses the work of Bowlby and Ainsworth on the mother-child relationship. His book takes you to the first discussions of how sick children were treated (mostly by isolation) to the current views of the critical role of parental involvement. Experiencing abandonment at a youthful age is at the core of many psychological disorders that manifest in adulthood. He describes the difficulty experienced when children cannot form attachments that make them feel secure and safe. Karen has put together the historical and research discoveries that have made us aware of the truth; as Wordsworth said, "The child is father to the man." In it we can clearly see clues to the origin of why an individual may be susceptible to traumatization.

It is agreeably written, and the brilliant organization of the material is truly a private guide through a mountain of material.

Stratheaern, L., Jian, L., Fongay, P., & Montague, P. R. (2008). What's in a smile? Maternal responses to infant facial cues. *Pediatrics* 122:40–51.

Key dopamine-associated reward processing regions of the brain were activated when mothers viewed their own infant's face compared with an unknown infant's face. These included ventral tegmental area/substantia nigra regions (reward areas of the brain), the striatum, and frontal lobe regions involved with emotion processing (medial prefrontal, anterior cingulated, and insula cortex), cognition (dorsolateral prefrontal cortex), and motor behavioral outputs (motivation to action areas of the brain). Happy, but not neutral or sad, infant faces activated nigrostriatal brain regions interconnected by dopaminergic neurons, including the substantia nigra and dorsal putamen. These data support the rewarding and motivating power of an infant's smile.

Field, T. (2002). Infants' need for touch. *Hum. Dev.* 45:100–103.

In the extremes of touch, significant effects on growth, development, and emotional well-being were clearly evident. Extreme cases can be seen in the Romanian orphanages where children achieved half their expected height due to touch deprivation. Their cognitive and emotional development had also been significantly delayed by the lack of physical stimulation. On the other hand, using massage therapy with preterm infants can facilitate growth. Massage enhances weight gain and development, and with normal infants, facilitates sleep, reduces irritability, and enhances performance. (See also *Trauma touch therapy*, www.csha.net.)

Chemtob, C. M., Nomura, Y., & Abramovitz, R. A. (2008). Impact of conjoined exposure to the World Trade Center attacks and to other traumatic events on the behavioral problems of preschool children. *Arch. Pediatr. Adolesc. Med.* 162:126–133.

Preschoolers who witnessed the September 11 attack on the World Trade Center or saw its victims were at high risk for developing lingering emotional and behavioral problems if—and only if—they had had a previous frightening experience. These authors conclude that the additive effects of trauma exposure are consistent with the hypothesis of kindling. They recommend a more vigorous outreach to trauma-exposed preschool children.

Chapter 7: Disrupting a Traumatization

Monfils, M-H., Cowansage, K. K., Klann, E., LeDoux, J. E. (2009). Extinction-reconsolidation roundaries: Key to persistent attenuation of fear memories. *Science*. 324: 951–955.
Two paradigms (blockade of reconsolidation and extinction) have been used in the laboratory to reduce acquired fear. Unfortunately, their clinical efficiency is limited: reconsolidation blockade requires potentially toxic drugs and extinction is not permanent. In this experiment, extinction training (the rapid repetition of the CS without the UFS) was applied within the reconsolidation window (after the memory is rendered unstable by presenting an isolated retrieval trial). This procedure permanently attenuated the fear memory in a way completely different than normal extinction training. This article is consistent with the hypothesis suggested in this book.

Levine, P. (1997). *Waking the tiger. Healing trauma*. Berkeley, CA: North Atlantic Books.
Levine believes that traumatic memories are not caused by the event itself, but rather from the frozen residue of energy that has not been resolved and discharged. For him, a traumatized human must discharge all the energy mobilized to deal with the threat or he or she will become a victim of trauma. How this is accomplished is described in Levine's book. He demonstrates how his method, somatic experiencing, can be used to heal traumatization.

Ogden, P., Minton, K., & Pain, C. (2006). *Trauma and the body: A sensorimotor approach to psychotherapy*. New York, NY: W.W. Norton & Co.
Trauma is trapped not only in the mind, but also in the body. Ogden and coworkers demonstrate that a traumatic memory can be activated just by the use of body sensations. The book's main thesis is that by accessing the body-centered experience of the trauma, we can explore without fear and hopefully free our minds from the seemingly permanently encoded moment. It is an extremely well-thought-out and organized book and is offered as another tool for therapists of all orientations.

Baddeley, A. (1998). Recent developments in working memory. *Curr. Opin. Neurobiol.* 8:234–238.
The Baddeley and Hitch model assumes an attentional control system, a central executive, which operates in conjunction with two subsidiary systems, the phonological loop and the visual-spatial sketchpad. Functional imaging studies suggest that encoding occurs on the left side of the brain and retrieval on the right side of the brain. Recall that the right amygdala

is involved with traumatization. This article is the basis for the distraction processes used to disrupt working memory. Thus, we need to divert attention and disrupt the visual and auditory cues attending a traumatic event.

A question arises as to whether all information brought into working memory becomes available to conscious awareness. In the model described in this book, it is speculated that retrieval of subconscious stimuli enters working memory en route to the amygdala, but does not reach awareness. Nonetheless, the information activates glutamate pathways in the amygdala that tie it to other components. See also *working memory* in Wikipedia (http://en.wikipedia.org/wiki/working_ memory) for a discussion of its location, executive function, and other details.

Aston-Jones, G., Akaoka, H., Charlety, P., & Chouvet, G. (1991). Serotonin selectively attenuates glutamate-evoked activation of noradrenergic locus coeruleus neurons. *J. Neurosci.* 11:760–769.

The nucleus of the locus coeruleus receives a dense innervation of serotonergic fibers. Serotonin (5HT2A) receptors appear to selectively inhibit excitatory neurons via action on GABA-releasing neurons. Thus, serotonin inhibits those neurons that are activated by glutamate from releasing norepinephrine.

Lake, D. (2008). *Acceptance tapping—A powerful EFT treatment for severe compulsive disorders and bulimia.* Retrieved from www.eftuniverse.com

This article describes the use of self-tapping during activation of a compulsive act. We would term this self-havening. The idea is to have the brain experience havening each and every time the compulsive drive is present. Over time, it is postulated that this drive can be extinguished. However, like addictive behaviors, where stopping a specific substance from being abused is shifted to another substance, compulsive behaviors may also be shifted to another act. The key is to downregulate the brain so that all compulsive activities cease. If the distress that motivates this behavior is due to a trauma, havening the traumatization may have beneficial effects.

Spoont, M. (1992). Modulatory role of serotonin in neural information processing: Implications for human psychopathology. *Psychol. Bull.* 112:330–350.

This article describes the anatomy and physiology of the serotonin system in humans and explores the role of serotonin as a modulator of dopamine activity. In the case of the amygdala, the same argument can be made for the interaction of serotonin, norepinephrine, and dopamine. In the appetitive system, serotonin abolishes dopamaine-driven food-seeking behavior. No learning is necessary to stop the food-seeking behavior, just the rise of serotonin accomplished by consuming food. In the aversive system, the elevated levels of serotonin diminish salience and vigilance.

Field, T., Hernandez-Reif, M., Diego, M., Schanberg, S., & Kuhn, C. (2005). Cortisol decreases and serotonin and dopamine increase following massage therapy. *Int. J. Neurosci.* 115:1397–1413.

Field, T., Diego, M., & Hernandez-Reif, M. (2005). Massage therapy research. *Dev. Rev.* 27:75–89.

To date, it has been shown that stimulating pressure receptors under the skin increases the tone of the vagus nerve and causes a decrease in heart rate, and a change in voice and facial expression of depressed individuals. Vagal nerve stimulation has been shown to help with depression and with the prevention of seizures. Serotonin and dopamine levels are increased and cortisol levels decreased during massage.

Chapter 8: Havening

Dietrich, A. M., Baranowsky, A. B., Devich-Navarro, M., Gentry, J. E., Harris, J., & Figley, C. R. (2000). A review of alternative approaches to the treatment of post-traumatic sequelae. *Traumatology* 6:251–271.

This landmark but sometimes criticized paper describes and compares different alternative approaches to the treatment of PTSD. These methods included Trauma Recovery Institute method, trauma incident reduction, visual/kinesthetic disassociation, and Thought Field Therapy (TFT). All these methods, except TFT, have been validated. The authors concluded that alternative therapies must withstand careful scrutiny, and we should discard or revise those that fail to maintain the standards of efficacy and safety.

Callahan, R., & Callahan, J. (2000). *Stop the nightmares of trauma.* Chapel Hill, NC: Professional Press.

Callahan, R., & Trubo, R. (2002). *Tapping the healer within. Using Thought Field Therapy to instantly conquer your fears, anxieties and emotional distress.* New York, NY: McGraw-Hill.

While CT-TFT has been seriously criticized on both a theoretical and methodological basis, it does work. In his book *Thought Field Therapy*, Roger Callahan correctly states that most of human suffering, certainly in first world countries, is due to emotional traumatization. According to Callahan, a thought field is the energy generated when you think of a traumatic event from your life. It is perturbed due to blockages in the flow of energy along meridians. This analysis relies on traditional Chinese medicine, which views the body as infused with energy flowing along pathways called meridians.

These meridians have points along their path called acupoints where traditional Chinese physicians place needles to encourage a healthier flow of energy. Thought Field Therapy consists of bringing the memory of the event to mind and then, depending on the problem that presents, tapping on specific but different acupoints. As peculiar as this seems, it is extremely successful in relieving a host of problems that are the consequences of traumatization, such as phobias, PTSD, pathological emotions, and others. It is to Dr. Callahan's credit, despite many criticisms of this approach, that he has persevered and helped many live without the distress. One major concern about his methods involves his costly advanced training course, called Voice Technology (see Pignotti, M. (2004). Callahan fails to meet the burden of proof for Thought Field Therapy claims. *J. Clin. Psychol.* 61:251–255, and http://www.integrative-clearing.com.au/tft_split.html).

Church, D. (2010). The treatment of combat trauma using EFT (Emotional Freedom Techniques): A pilot protocol. *Traumatology*, 16(1): 55–65.

A pilot program using 11 veterans and family members who were assessed for PTSD and treated with a brief (five days) EFT. EFT is an exposure therapy using mild sensory input. One-year follow-up on seven of the participants showed they no longer met criteria for PTSD. This suggests that EFT can be an effective postdeployment intervention.

Craig, G. www.eftuniverse.com

This Web site offers a free download of Gary Craig's approach to psychological problems. While he also ascribes the healing power of tapping to meridians and energy fields, his ideas are grounded in a sophisticated clinical approach. This web site should be read by anyone wishing to do this form of therapy. In addition, Gary has a free newsletter providing tips and case studies to help those who practice what he calls Emotional Freedom Techniques (EFT). This model differs from TFT in several ways. (See http://www.integrative-clearing.com.au/eft/eft_and_tft.html for a detailed analysis.) In EFT, the problem is activated by a setup phrase that incorporates a component of the event, and he has one set of tapping points.

The theoretical model described in our book does not provide an explanation for many of the case studies that are described in his newsletters. Indeed, some are downright astonishing.

Gary states that we should try this approach on every problem encountered, as we have nothing to lose and potentially a cure to be gained. Gary has a disclaimer about not "going where you don't belong," meaning that seriously ill individuals should be treated by professional health care providers.

Kim, J., Lee, S, Park, K, Hong, I., Song, B., Son, G., Park, H., Kim, W. R., Park, E, Choe, H. K, Kim, H., Lee, C., Sun, W., Kim, K, Shin, KS. & Choi, S. (2007). Amygdala depotentiation and fear extinction. *Proceed. Nat. Acad. Sci.* 104(52): 20955–20960.

This paper is of critical importance in understanding the effect of havening on encoded memories. It shows that application of low frequency pulses to an in vitro preparation of rat amygdala, wherein the rat had been conditioned to an auditory stimulus, produced depotentiation of AMPA receptors in the thalamo-amygdala pathway. This depotentiation caused the AMPA receptor to become internalized within the post-synaptic amygdala neuron preventing further downstream activation.

Chapter 9: A Brief Introduction to Psychosensory Therapy

Fellows, D., Barnes, K., & Wilkinson, S. (2004). Aromatherapy and massage for symptom relief in patients with cancer. *Cochrane Database Syst. Rev.* 2:CD00287.

The most consistently found effect of massage or aromatherapy was on anxiety. Four trials (207 patients) measuring anxiety detected a reduction in postinterventions, with benefits of 19 to 32% reported.

Cottingham, J. T. (1985). *Healing through touch. A history and review of the physiological evidence.* Boulder, CO: Rolf Institute.

The term *somatic* (body) *techniques* is used to describe a range of techniques that involve touching the body. Healing through touch goes back more than the 5,000 years of recorded history. Prehistoric cave paintings portray the laying on of hands for the sick and injured. It is intended for the curious reader and serious student who would like to understand the historical and Cottingham's view of the theoretical basis of these therapies.

Eden, D., with D. Feinstein. (1998). *Energy medicine.* New York, NY: Tarcher/The Penguin Group USA.

Donna Eden sees the world in an extraordinary way. She is able to visualize energy fields that surround people. Guided by her senses, she performs healing that would be considered just this side of miraculous. For her, the body is suffused with visible energy. The energy must flow unimpeded for the body to function normally. The healing system she describes is internally consistent, albeit invisible to most, untouchable, and unknowable, except for a few well-tuned individuals. This book describes many approaches to alter energy for health, including breathing, posture, movement, massage, and nontouch healing. All involve the interaction of different energy systems within our bodies. In the final analysis, this is a book about subtle energy, the rhythms that impact on our lives (such as the seasons), and how we can open our awareness to these energies. Donna Eden knows to the depth of her soul that all things in the universe are connected.

Feinstein, D., Eden, D., & Craig, G. (2005). *The promise of energy psychology.* New York, NY: Jeremy P. Tarcher/The Penguin Group USA.

This book phenomenally outlines current thinking in the field of energy psychology for those who appreciate and feel comfortable with the Eastern model.

Association for Comprehensive Energy Psychology (ACEP). www.EnergyPsych.org

ACEP is an international nonprofit organization of licensed mental health professionals and allied energy health practitioners dedicated to developing and applying energy psychology methods for the treatment of those suffering from emotional challenges such as addictions, compulsions, anxiety, depression, limiting beliefs, personality disorders, phobias, stress, and trauma. Energy psychology interventions address the human vibrational matrix of three major interacting systems:

Energy pathways—meridians and related acupoints

Energy centers—chakras

Energy systems—the human biofield that envelops the body

ACEP seeks to establish the credibility and effectiveness of energy psychology through its programs of certification, education, ethics, humanitarian aid, and research.

International scope of ACEP. ACEP members come from more than 50 countries around the globe, including the western hemisphere, Europe, Africa, the Middle East, Australia, and the Pacific Rim. Twenty-two countries were represented at the 2008 annual international conference in Albuquerque, New Mexico.

ACEP certification program. ACEP sponsors a two-track certification program aimed at helping practitioners to amplify their credibility, upgrade their energy psychology skills, and rise to their peak potential. The tracks are:

- DCEP (Diplomat, Comprehensive Energy Psychology) for licensed mental health professionals, or the international equivalent.
- CEHP (Certified Energy Health Practitioner) for allied health and human service practitioners and nonlicensed mental health professionals and academics. Candidates must complete home study modules available online, participate in workshops focused on technical and ethical competence, and demonstrate treatment proficiency under the guidance of an ACEP certification consultant.

This organization holds conferences and exposes those interested to vendors who offer a variety of systems and techniques to modify these energy fields. I have attended two conferences and found the individuals open to exploration of the ideas found in traditional Chinese medicine.

Benson, H. (1976). *The relaxation response.* New York, NY: HarperTorch.

This landmark book describes the effects of relaxation on several physiological parameters. For an up-to-date review of this research go to www.RelaxationResponse.org.

Appendix J: Glossary

afferents: Axons that enter an area of the brain from elsewhere. *See* efferents.

AMPA receptor: A class of glutamate receptor involved in memory and learning. See http://en.Wikipedia.org/wiki/Glutamate_Receptor.

amygdala: A paired group of nuclei in the temporal lobes of the brain affecting various aspects of memory (e.g., storage, retrieval, and associations), especially memory that is involved with emotional states.

BLC: The basolateral complex (BLC) of the amygdala. It is the location where affective memory is mediated, but it is not the location of memory. It is made up of the lateral nucleus, basolateral nucleus (BLA), and accessory basal nucleus, whose efferents activate the central nucleus and other brain areas, including the hippocampus and the medial prefrontal cortex.

central executive: The part of the brain that decides what we attend to.

complex content: A combination of unimodal sensory input and other related aspects of the event, which can include color, size, speed, visceral sensations, and pain.

conditioned response: The learned response to a neutral stimulus when it is paired with an unconditioned stimulus.

conscious: Information of which we are self-aware.

context: The surroundings unrelated to content, e.g. the place the event occurs.

cortisol: A hormone secreted by the adrenal gland. It influences the immune system, the body's electrolytes, glucose levels, and the ability to learn and remember, and has a diurnal variation, peaking around 6.00 a.m. and bottoming out around 4.00 p.m. It appears to be necessary for the traumatic encoding of emotional events.

declarative memory: Knowledge to which we have conscious access, such as events in our lives and facts we have learned.

defensive rage: A response to fear when fighting or fleeing is not an option. It involves a clenched jaw, tight neck muscles, flared nostrils, dilated pupils, and an arched back.

depotentiation: The removal of a receptor after activation during memory recall. In the case of activated glutamate receptor, low-frequency electrical (1 to 5 Hz) stimulation accomplishes this.

dissociation: The process by which a component of memory is stored such that its accessibility by conscious thought is prevented.

distraction: The use of cognitive, visual, and auditory input to displace the current content of working memory.

dopamine: Transmitted by efferents from the ventral tegmental area, this substance affects salience and vigilance, and motivates and drives motoric action.

dorsal striatum: Infracortical elements that include the caudate, putamen, and the fundus.

dysregulation: A medical term for disordered regulation of a homeostatic process leading to disease.

efferents: Axons that leave an area of the brain and are connected to another area. *See* afferents.

EFT: Emotional Freedom Techniques (see www.eftuniverse.com). A psychosensory therapy useful for a wide range of problems. It involves exposure to a psychological or physical problem followed by mild sensory stimulation.

encoding: The process of consolidating a memory in the brain and all the experiences occurring with that event.

extrasensory response: An unbidden, hardwired, or learned response to sensory input that has meaning to the individual.

fear: A state of motivation that is aroused by certain specific stimuli. It produces a coordinated physiological response to deal with a perceived threat and normally gives rise to freezing, escape, or defensive behavior.

fear conditioning: The process by which a neutral stimulus is paired with an unconditioned fear stimulus. After several pairings, presentation of the neutral stimulus leads to the production of a fear response.

fight or flight: A moment of fear resulting in elevated levels of dopamine, norepinephrine, cortisol, and epinephrine. It is associated with increased muscular strength, increased oxygen consumption, and other heightened physiological processes designed to improve the chances of survival when threatened by a predator.

flaccidity: A state of skeletal muscular inactivity. Fainting, in the presence of a powerful emotional stimulus, is an example.

freeze: A moment of fear. Similar to vigilance, it allows for assessment and focus and makes the individual motionless.

freeze discharge: After being pursued and caught by a predator, an animal may respond by becoming flaccid. The freeze response mimics death. In some cases, if the animal survives, it begins to tremble in a manner much like running. Peter Levine feels that it is this retained memory of flight that needs to be discharged to treat traumatization.

GABA: Gamma-amino butyric acid. This neurochemical inhibits other neurons and is the counter to glutamate.

gamut procedure: Various cognitive, auditory, and physical maneuvers, such as tapping, humming a song, counting, and eye movements that act to displace the current content of working memory.

glutamate: An excitatory neurochemical. The disruption (depotentiation) of activated AMPA receptors is postulated to occur during eye movement desensitization and reprocessing and havening.

hardwired: A response that does not need to be learned. Under appropriate conditions, hardwired responses to stimuli activate systems that are critical to survival.

havening therapy: A form of therapy that seeks to disrupt the encoded relationship between the emotional and cognitive portion of a traumatic memory. Therapy requires activation of the BLC, using either a felt sense or conscious thought, and is followed by havening touch, eye movements, tapping, and distraction.

havening touch: Touch that increases the amplitude of the low-frequency electrical delta wave. It is a firm but gentle touch that is hardwired to produce comfort and make us feel safe.

hippocampus: An area close to the amygdala that processes contextual and other cortically processed information and is critical for storage and retrieval of declarative memory.

homeostasis: This term refers to the process that returns the brain's electrical and neurochemical landscape to a previously preset level.

homeostatic: The baseline levels of neurochemicals that the body returns to after experiencing a stressor.

inescapable stress: A circumstance that cannot be avoided, producing an adaptive response by the organism. This adaptive response can turn maladaptive.

kindling: The sensitization of the brain by previous experiences that make it more susceptible to traumatization. In neurology, it is defined as lowering the threshold to seizures.

landscape: The levels of brain neurochemicals that are the result of the interaction between what is inherent and what is environmental, between what has already passed and what is currently present.

limbic system: A group of interconnected brain structures whose function is to improve our chances for survival. Motivation, emotion and learning are modulated here.

locus coeruleus: Located in the brainstem, this area is the source of norepinephrine efferents.

mirror neurons: A class of neurons that discharges during both observation and experiencing an action or emotion.

mammillary body: Located at the end of the fornix, it sends signals to the anterior and dorsomedial nuclei in the thalamus and is involved with the processing of recognition memory.

neuromodulators: Chemicals that set steady-state levels of neuronal activity.

neurotransmitters: Chemicals, such as glutamate, that are released as the result of stimuli.

nondeclarative memory: Memory that involves skills and habits, conditioned reflexes, and emotional associations. Also called procedural memory, memories stored here cannot be told in a narrative form.

norepinephrine: Transmitted by efferents from the locus coeruleus, this neurochemical affects almost the entire cortical and sub-cortical structures. It has wide-ranging physiological and psychological functions.

nucleus accumbens: An area of the brain involved in motivated behavior and motoric action.

panic: An extremely excited state of mind and body that is not under conscious control.

panic attacks: An unprovoked activation of the brain that produces an extreme fear response.

parasympathetic nervous system: One of the coordinators of our body. It affects digestion, blood pressure, heart rate, and so on. The parasympathetic and sympathetic systems usually work in opposite directions, thus allowing for modulation of the body's functions.

phobia: An inappropriate fear response, generated by the association of an unconditional fear stimulus with any other stimulus.

phonological loop: The part of working memory that rehearses verbal information.

physicalism: The belief that physical symptoms have a physical cause.

potentiation: Refers to the increase in magnitude of a glutamate-driven post-synaptic response.

prefrontal cortex: The front part of the brain used for evaluation and assessment and intimately connected to the emotional system, including the amygdala. It has several subcomponents that perform different functions. See http://en.Wikipedia.org/wiki/Prefrontal_cortex.

procedural memory: The earliest form of memory that helps us get food to our mouths and learn to walk. It is also involved with emotional learning.

psychopharmacotherapy: The use of drugs to alter dysfunctional behavior, mood and thinking.

psychosensory therapy: The application of sensory input on either an activated mind or a quiet mind designed to alter brain functioning. Psychosensory stimuli can change the brain temporarily or permanently.

psychosocial: Aspects of attachment related to culture and society, such as the sense of belonging, acceptance, and being appreciated.

psychotherapy: The treatment of a mental or emotional disorder or of related bodily ills by psychological means.

reactive emotions: Fear and defensive rage are hardwired and innate emotions that are produced by threatening stimuli.

reflective emotions: These require assessment of our circumstances, such as feelings of revenge, guilt, and hatred.

resilience: The ability of a body to recover it original state after a stressor has modified it.

routine emotions: These arise as a natural consequence to our circumstances, such as happiness and sadness.

salience: A state where an object becomes of great importance at that moment.

sensation: Activation of a receptor organ by a stimulus, including thought. This activation is converted to a common electro-chemical language and processed.

serotonin: A neurochemical that is transmitted by efferents from the brain stem raphe nuclei and spread to certain areas, most notably the frontal cortex, amygdala, hippocampus, the locus coeruleus and the nucleus accumbens. It is speculated that it carries the release of GABA in the amygdala and generates a low frequency wave.

somatic experiencing®: A therapeutic intervention that involves physiological arousal followed by an imaginary escape to a safe place.

somatization: The encoding of a somatosensory or visceral component of a traumatizing event that is experienced after the traumatic moment has passed.

somatosensory: Sensed in the body.

stimulus (pl. stimuli): An event that triggers a sensory response.

storage: The process by which a component of an event is consolidated in the brain such that retrieval can occur.

stress: A change of our internal or external environment that alters homeostasis.

subconscious: Mental content, generated by internal or external stimuli, that is not consciously registered but may nonetheless stimulate somatic symptoms and affect arousal.

SUD score: Subjective unit of distress (SUD). A patient-evaluated sense of self-distress. An 11-point scoring scale from 0 to 10, where 0 is no distress and 10 is extreme distress.

sympathetic nervous system: The coordinator of the flight-or-flight response. It affects every organ because the neurochemicals secreted by this system enter the bloodstream. The neurochemicals involved, epinephrine and cortisol, are secreted by the adrenal gland.

TFT: Thought Field Therapy (see www.tftrx.com). A psychosensory therapy developed by Dr. Roger Callahan. Like havening, EFT, and eye movement desensitization and reprocessing, it is an exposure therapy with mild sensory stimulation afforded by touch and other activities.

thalamus: The post office of the brain where sensory input is parceled to other parts of the brain for interpretation and perception generation.

thanatosis: Flaccidity. Playing dead. A state where sensory input is blocked so that it does not reach consciousness.

traditional Chinese medicine: The use of herbs, nutrition, acupuncture, and meditation to help the body heal.

transduced stimulus: The result of transduction; that is, information contained in a stimulus is converted into another form.

transduction: The process of conversion of one type of signal to another.

traumatic memory: A memory composed of four components: cognitive, emotional, autonomic, and somatosensory. These components have a complex relationship. The emotional component is the glue that ties these components together. A traumatic memory can be encoded when an emotional event with the appropriate meaning, landscape, and perceived inescapability occurs.

traumatized: Encoded as a traumatization.

unconditioned fear stimuli (UFS): Stimuli that provoke a fear response that does not require learning, e.g., an eye blink as an object unexpectedly enters the visual field at close range.

unconditioned response: An automatic response to an unconditioned stimulus.

unconditioned stimulus: A pattern that elicits a response without prior learning.

unimodal content: The object or thought directly associated with an unconditioned stimulus, e.g. a gun.

vasomotor system: Regulates the size of blood vessels and hence the flow through them. Blushing is a vasomotor response where blood vessels of the face dilate.

vigilance: A heightened state of mind and body, alertness.

visual-spatial sketch pad: Part of working memory that is engaged when performing spartial tasks (judging distance) or visual ones (counting pennies on the table).

working memory: An area in the frontal cortex that holds thoughts and ideas so that they may be manipulated and acted upon.

Index

T - #0059 - 021020 - C0 - 229/152/13 - PB - 9781138872615